Thumb

a Softy

My Struggle

Wendell Gee

First paperback edition October 2020

ISBN: 9798686594838

4LJ

Contents

1 Call me Wendell

Gently rolling my scrotum between thumb and forefinger, like an old Italian Nonna fashioning pasta for her family on an ancient oak table in the shade of a wizened olive tree.
My first self-examination in 12 years was finally, paying my often ignored orchids the attention they so rightly deserved.

I had the house to myself, Zero 7 on shuffle, the heady perfume of Lynx Africa wafting in on the steam from the en-suite and my recently cleaned balls doing a jig between my fingers on the edge of the bed.

I was amazed at how much further I could stretch my scrotum after a hot shower. I reached for my phone and tapped torch. With it shining through the gossamer thin membrane, I marvelled at the beautiful roadmap of tiny veins it revealed. I wondered if I could read newsprint through it if I really pulled hard. I couldn't, but then my wife's bedtime novel did have very small print!

Concentrate on the job in hand I told myself, it's time to check my right nut. Maybe slightly larger than the left, my right nut hung a little lower and had a tiny freckle just right of centre, when looking at them together though, they still looked a matching pair to me.

Easing my testical forward away from my arsehole, I pinched the back of the sac and slowly wiggled my fingers forwards. FUCK! What was that?

My hands flew apart into the air and I fell back on the bed, like I'd just touched a live wire. Noooo…! It couldn't be…! Fuck Shit Wank Tit Cunt Bum Arsehole! I wasn't meant to find anything, that was not in the script, this was just supposed to be an excuse for me to play with my balls!
'Ignore it, it'll be nothing.' I thought.
No I couldn't, that wasn't the grown up thing to do. How long had it been there? Why hadn't I felt it before? I didn't know. Maybe if I hadn't been such a caring, selfless lover, always putting my girlfriends sexual needs ahead of my own, I might have caught this earlier. I should have spent more time exploring and worshipping my body, instead of just theirs.

My eyes tightly closed and teeth gritted, I tentatively reached my finger towards the lump again, slowly lowering it to the skins surface. 'No that's my bum-hole!' I recoiled.
I opened my eyes, as if that would help my accuracy, my fingertip slowly descending for a second landing, there it was, found it! Like a peanut sized lump of worry, it was hard and smooth and moved with my stretched ball sack skin.

Not wanting to accept its existence, I still had to see it. I stood and reached for my T-shirt from the bed, pulling it over my head as I stepped towards the dressing table. If I was going to suddenly collapse into a bollock cancer induced coma, at least my top half would be covered and I'd retain a little dignity.

The small, round make-up mirror opened with a sudden jolt, sending a powder cloud across the dressing table and on to the carpet below. That was no good, looking around, I realised the full-length mirror on the wall was the only option left to me. I sat on the floor facing it, a shaking, sweating, dying man looking back at me.

Like a dog with worms, I shimmied my arse closer and closer to my reflection, leaning back, I raised my legs either side of the mirror and planted my feet on the wall.

My aging eyes couldn't really focus on the already fuzzy scene, I leaned forward, squinting, I could see all my bits but not in enough detail. Reluctantly I shimmied back a bit, swung my knees over and onto all fours, then padded over to the bedside drawers like a puppy, in search of my £1.99 reading glasses.

Pushing a few photos of my old Karmann Ghia to the back of the drawer and brushing aside a packet of Mates ribbed, that went out of date in 2004, one spectacle arm and half a lens revealed itself to me. I pulled the arm and with the glasses came my knotted broken Apple headphones and a magnetic bulldog clip. After 30 seconds of untangling they were free, I put the glasses on my forehead and pushed the drawer shut, I turned for the mirror, then I thought,
'I haven't seen my old car pictures for ages.'
I retrieved them back out of the drawer and left them on the bed to look at later. I turned again for the mirror, like Dick Wittington, then I thought,
'They would be neater and wouldn't get bent if I used the magnetic bulldog clip to stick them to the iron bed frame.'
The photos snapped to the upright with a pleasing click, a magnet always brought me joy, with its scientific magic, however menial the job you ask it to do. I'd made sure the picture on top, was the car taken from the side, so that you could see the boot of the car too, always the best angle for a Karmann Ghia I thought…Hold on, I think I'm procrastinating, I've my bollock lump to see.

Back at the mirror I assumed the smear-test position again,
this time bespectacled. I parted my sparse pubic-lawn hairs,
I could see nothing obvious but there did seem to be a slight
discolouration around the lump, a feint greying of the skin. I
had seen enough, I struggled backwards and up, still shaking I
pulled my pants on.

I looked back towards the mirror and my heart sank even lower,
I spotted two great shiny footprints on the eggshell paint, either
side of the frame! 'How would I explain that to the wife?'

'Is this it? Was that my life all over?'
I sat staring trance like at the shiny footprints for hours, maybe
just minutes, probably only seconds.
'Had I achieved all I wanted from my life?'
I hadn't been this close to deaths door since I was five or six
years old.

2 70s

To set the scene, it was Essex in the early 70s, my Mum had parked outside her favourite garden centre on the hill in Hockley, where we lived. Our white Renault 16 was our playroom for the couple of minutes she said she'd be gone.

There were no namby-pamby nanny-state child seats in those days, just big, black vinyl bench seats front and back. As soon as Mum was out of sight, I jumped into the front and my little brother Pip laughed, I sat behind the wheel like mummy does, broom brooming and pretending to steer. Mum always pulls that black handle thing like this, I thought, releasing the handbrake. The car started rolling forward, slowly at first then faster and faster as the hill steepened, I am loving this!

As the houses passed in a blur, all of a sudden a ruddy, red faced, old man in a cap appeared at the window running next to the car, his little legs struggling to keep up. He was trying to open the door but the child locks were on. He was shouting, 'Open the window!'
I thought, 'Uh Oh, I'm in trouble.'
I wound the window down to talk to him, he jumped through the window into the car, flying across me, his legs flailing

outside. He was obviously hoping to find the handbrake in the middle of the car as usual, not in a 1970s French car!
'What did you do? What did you touch?' He kept shouting.
I pointed to the pistol-gripped handbrake in the foot well, just to the front of the driver's door.

I was still giggling as we gradually rolled to a stop. The funny red man was really gasping, I think he'd been holding his breath. He pushed himself out of the car and stood with his hands on knees. The noise of his gasping being replaced by Mum's screams at us, as she ran down the hill. I hurriedly tried to get into the back seats, but she caught me in the act, I thought I'm going to have to take the blame for this one.

I have nothing but fond memories of my early years and I always felt loved, probably because I was such a sweet, well behaved little boy. Although when I put gravel up my nose because it felt like a big, hard bogey, I think I did get a bit of a telling off. I tried blaming my one year old brother Pip, that was funny but a trip to the doctor was needed to get the stone out.

When I set alight the hedge around the field opposite our house and watched the firemen fighting the fire, their engines parked right in front of our garden with their lights flashing, that was exciting. There were big boys who were smoking and they had dropped a box of matches minutes before, I managed to get them blame for the whole thing. I only lit one match, I wanted to watch a little twig burn. I thought it would just smoulder, like one of Mum's cigarettes, but as it took it was too scary to hold, so I threw it under the hedge, thinking, 'That'll put it out!

When the Policeman asked me if I'd seen anything, not blaming them directly, I did say that I saw some boys smoking and told him which way they went.

To get me back, the big boys kidnapped me and my friend Peter a few days later, holding us hostage on a building site for what seemed hours. When they got bored and went home for their tea, to stop us escaping they pissed a puddle across the doorway. It was the only exit and they said we'd die if we touched it. It was at least half an hour before we'd plucked up enough courage to jump the piss puddle. We discussed it at length and decided that it wouldn't kill us. It all seems funny now.

Dad's work moved from Southend, to Ipswich and we settled in East Bergholt. I was too young to have an opinion on the move but remember being excited, the thought of having trees to climb and straw bails after harvest to make great dens with. We lived in the middle of an estate in Hockley, but now I could see fields and trees to play in from my bedroom window.

I made friends with Peter on my first day at the new school, he only lived 10 doors away on my estate in an identical house and had a little brother the same age as mine. His Mum was Spanish and his Dad Iranian, he owned a shipping company and had a photo of his container ship on the wall.

My Dad was very laid back, I can never remember a raised voice when I was little, so it was a shock when Peter had been naughty and his Mum threatened to tell his Dad, he shat himself. He was on his knees begging for her not to tell him, he put the fear of God into me too. And it was the fear of God because he was a Christian Iranian! We only lived there for just over a year, then we were on the move again.

I never met my Grandads, they didn't hang around for my arrival. Mum's Dad was a crane driver in the London docks, the one day he was helping out on the ground he got crushed by a crate, breaking his back and putting him in a wheelchair. Dad's Dad knew I was on the way and that he was going to be a Grandad, but died a couple of months before I was born. I did have two Nans though, Nanny Kim and Nanny Car. Nanny Kim had a half blind Poodle called Kim and Nanny Car had a car, a green Skoda. Nanny Kim died and Mum, being an only child, inherited everything.

This enabled us to buy a massive four bedroom house with an in and out driveway not far away. It was in a tiny hamlet of only about 50 dwellings and we were opposite the church in its centre. We all had bigger bedrooms, Dad also got a double garage, study and a recording studio. Mum got a large kitchen, room for her to paint and knot her Macramé and a large, blank garden to work her magic on. All this was great, but I'd still rather have my Nan back.

We kept in touch with Peter and family, us kids were all the same ages and our Mums always got on which helped. We invited them to see our new house, it was only three or four miles away from them and I couldn't wait to see Peter's face when he saw the size of my bedroom and our garden. They came over quite often and we played and explored the fields and country lanes, one day Pete said that he had moved too.

When we went to their house, we couldn't believe it, we couldn't actually see his house from the road. His front garden was 22 acres of parkland and had cows grazing in it, his drive was half a mile long. When we got to the house, there was a roundabout that wouldn't look out of place on the A12. A lake to one side and a swimming pool the other, next to the walled garden just before you get to the stable block.

Pete showed me round, there was a Kitchen the size of our whole house, a back staircase and a main sweeping staircase up to the six main Bedrooms, it was like a film set.
He opened the first door at the bottom of the stairs,
'This is the Dining Room,' he opened the next door,

'This is the grown ups Dining Room, we're only allowed in here
at Christmas.'
The next door was the Lounge with double doors leading to
a massive Sun Room with wicker chairs, overlooking the pool.
Back through the Kitchen, there was a door to the Cellar and
a two Bedroom Annex, with its own Kitchen and Lounge, this
was for his Nan.

Upstairs all the Bedrooms, as I peaked around the doors, looked
more or less the same. The best door was on the landing, I
thought it was the airing cupboard. It hid a twisty little staircase,
that led to three further rooms under the eaves, on the second
floor. It was here we spent most of our time, away from the
grown ups, it had sloping ceilings and dormer windows from
which we could survey our new Play Palace and its grounds.

Many summers were spent at the big house, I particularly
remember the summer of 1977 just after Elvis died. I didn't
really know of him before but every morning they played one
of his films, and we all watched transfixed. We'd found a Deity
to worship, someone cool! No longer would I be listening to
John Inman singing Teddy Bears Picnic and The Sailor With
The Navy Blue Eyes. Thanks for the album Nan, but I'm too
old for that now, I'm into The King.

All the kids tried to do the Elvis hair, Pete being of Spanish
and Iranian decent had thick black hair, perfect for being styled
into a Quiff and Duck's Arse. He had the leather jacket and
looked cool. I on the other hand, being of Lithuanian decent,
had wispy brown hair and looked like a pale, underfed, abducted
child, that had been found wandering on the moors.

My other main memory of those kids happened a few years
later, Pete's brother who was about 14, had taken his dad's car
and turned up at our house asking if we wanted to go for a
drive? Pip was really up for it, he always did have a naughty

streak, I on the other hand being older and a bit more sensible warned him against the idea. Until I saw out of the window that it was his dad's best car. A Mercedes-Benz 600 lwb, the one we'd never been allowed in.

Being the driver of my 896cc Polo, I'd never experienced a 6-litre car before so I agreed to just a little poodle around the country lanes, what harm could it do? We were in the middle of Suffolk miles from anywhere, I'm sure no-one will see us.

It was when we were doing 135mph past the Shell garage at Capel St Mary on the A12, that I suggested we call it a day. We got home safely and no-one was any the wiser. Pete's brother on the other hand, finished his day by losing control of the car when he got home, driving it round the roundabout too fast and ending upside down in his dads lake. I bet he tore him a new arsehole when he got home.

As we moved house quite a bit I had three different primary schools. Each time, being introduced into an already bonded group of kids, I was always the new boy. The first two schools seemed fleeting visits and hold very few memories for me, but the third was different. A tiny Victorian village school in Suffolk, only 50 pupils in three classrooms, three dinner ladies and three teachers. A student-like, skinny young one, a curly haired, sweaty, pudding-like one and then there was Eunice the headmistress and my nemesis.

A vinegar-titted, candifloss-haired throw back to a time of gas lighting and shitting in a garden shed. Her powdery grey skin seemed excessive for the bony skull beneath and hung like curtains of misery, beyond her jaw line towards the stupid string of old lady pearls, hanging around her turkey neck. Always wearing a polo neck jumper, it strained under the weight of her oversized, obsolete, pendulous bosom. A bosom that had never nursed a child or entertained a lover's gaze.

Once I made the mistake of answering a question without putting my hand up, she stared at me and hissed,

'See me after Lunch!'

This was my invitation to her lunch time punishment. Being a three room school, extra tables were put out in the school hall for lunch and put away after. Everyone had vanished outside to play leaving just me and Eunice, she got a piece of chalk from the blackboard and drew a square on the floor, right in the middle of the hall.

'Sit there and not a word!' She said.

Every lunchtime and playtime for over a week I had to sit in her fucking square and on numerous occasions after, what a bitch!

My brother Pip suffered at the hands of Vinegar Tits too. After one lunch time a dinner lady complained to Eunice that a spoon had been bent. I think it was around the time that Uri Geller had appeared on telly for the first time, wowing us all with his trademark spoon bending illusions. Pip got the blame and the spoon was duly dispatched in a sealed envelope addressed to my Dad. In the envelope with the spoon was a letter, stating quite clearly that if the results of this unacceptable vandalism weren't rectified, he would be sent the bill for a replacement spoon. Dad just bent the spoon back and returned it in another envelope addressed 'Eunice.'

Living in the middle of a field and having to pass many fields on your way to anywhere that wasn't in a field, we had a great choice of fields to play in. I spotted a really exciting field one day whilst being driven out of our village, it had a World War 2 pill box slap bang in its centre. It was on the far edge of our little hamlet about 20 minutes bike ride away.

One half term we decided to explore the pill box, we had a packed lunch, bottle of Cream Soda to share and the golden corn was waist high. We moved along the fields edge until we had the shortest route across the corn, coincidently our path followed the telegraph wires between two poles. I made a point of saying to Pip, that we should follow the wires on the way back, retracing our footsteps, flattening as little crop as possible.

Having finished our sandwiches we started soldiering, keeping an eye out for any approaching Nazi bastards. We had a large branch sticking through the gun slot to shoot the Germans and our Captain Mainwaring attitude made us more than a match for any sausage eating Kraut. As we scoured the horizon, we saw a figure coming towards us. This was no Jew hating Nazi, this was more scary, this was the farmer who owned the field! Right from the outset he was on the attack.
'Come here you little Bastards!' He shouted.
'Come here or I'll stick this Fuckin pitch fork up ya arse!'
His aggression shocked us into surrender, we didn't even contemplate trying to make a run for it.

Our bikes had been dumped at the front of the field but he forced us at fork point in the opposite direction. His two pronged weapon directed us towards the road and the bungalow where he lived. His only words being muttered, over and over, 'Little Bastards, I'll Fuckin teach you, Bastards.'
Not the most eloquent adversary for two scared primary school kids, but we got his gist. As we approached his house the next door neighbour came out and approached us. Thank God, it was a teacher from school, the curly haired, sweaty, pudding-like one. She'd been watching us from her window and probably thought Mr. Giles didn't really have the social skills needed to deal with the situation. What with him being a fucking moronic, carrot-crunching farmer twat!

She took over control from Worzel, we told her our phone number and she called Dad, we all waited for him to come and sort it out. It was an awkward 10 minutes, standing, waiting, the pitch fork had been lowered on the pudding ones instructions but he still had hold of it, standing there with his fat gut and trouser legs tied with string. Dad came and took us home no problems there, he just thought it was funny that we were caught by a Farmer Giles!

A couple of days later we had a letter from the farmer, hand delivered. It said that having looked at the field, he requested that we pay £6.50 for the damage we had caused to his crop or he'll call the police. Dad replied tongue in cheek, saying that any further correspondence should be sent to his lawyer, giving the address of his friend in Ipswich who was a Solicitor. We heard no more from Farmer Giles.

I thought that was an end to the matter, until I got back to school. The curly haired, sweaty, pudding-like one had obviously told Eunice about the incident and in her Vinegar Titted little way, took me to one side and told me that even in the holidays I was still representing the school, and I had let the school down. I got another week sitting in her Fucking chalky square for something I did in the holidays!

It was at this school I had my first real, 'Foot in the Mouth' moment. The first day of term after a long glorious summer break, I had a spring in my step and was raring to go. We were now the oldest kids in school, top class, we got to sit on the back row. I strolled into the room past my mate John sitting at the front.

'Cheer up John, someone died?' I said, as he was looking a bit gloomy. I could feel everyone's eyes rolling to the back of their collective heads as I sat down. 'You do know his mum just died?' Someone whispered. How could I have known? I felt like shit, what a great start to the term.

Thankfully it was 25 years before I did the same thing again at
work. The marketing manager walked in, her head down and she
was wearing big sunglasses indoors, I wasn't going to let her get
away with that.

'Hey Film-star, can I have your autograph?' I jokingly quipped.
She tool off the glasses, her face a mess of wet mascara and
running nose, she'd obviously been crying.

'My d,d,dad died last n,n,night!' Sniff, sniff, 't,t,the police are all
over the h,house,' sniff, 'because they say it was an unexplained
death,' she mumbled.

Not being great at emotional shit, I got up and said that I'd
make her a nice, compassionate cup of tea, leaving her to
compose herself. As I passes by the blokes in the next office
I gave them a situation report, hoping that being a bit older,
they'd be better at grieving, middle-aged woman hugs and
understanding etc.

3 High

Big school was a real eye-opener, all of a sudden we were plucked from our quaint little Victorian village school with 50 pupils, to Hadleigh High, a modern, sprawling, bungalow school with 800. We'd gone from being the big fish in a twee little village pond, to minnows floundering around in a river of pubescent Piranha.

Our new peers walked with a chest-out swagger and had deep voices, hairy legs and attitude, that was just the girls. The one Indian kid we had in Year 5 even had a beard! My old year class of eight to ten kids was now six classes with 180, a daunting situation, but we soon settled in and found new soul mates.

Year 1 Form Head was an RE teacher as old as the bible itself, his big round tweed suit always covered in chalk dust, he insisted on using his hand instead of a board rubber. He never made eye contact or tried to stop the class chatting, he just carried on in his own little world mummbling and stumbling along.

Year 2 we had Mr Parker a Maths teacher, at first we thought he was a mini Hitler, a right little bully. His method of controlling the kids was to throw the wooden board rubber at whoever wasn't paying attention. It fucking hurt too. He soon calmed down when we grew taller than him and started returning the board rubber to him, faster and more accurately than he could, he stopped his bullying and ended up one of my favourite teachers.

It wasn't until Year 3 that I got into real trouble and nearly got suspended, it was all a complete misunderstanding. Our form tutor Mr Epilepsy was OK, by coincidence his wife was a teacher where my mum worked as a classroom helper and they were friends. My brother and I had the embarrassment of a Teacher from school coming round our house socially for dinner parties. To make matters worse, I was the one who had to give him the invitations in class in front of all my mates.

The misunderstanding happened when Skavva, Iggy and Me, being responsible, mature kids, were entrusted with clearing out an old storeroom, it was packed floor to ceiling with unused desks and chairs. It used to be where photography club was held before our time. After an hour or so of moving these desks snd chairs to another room, we found a door to some unused toilets on the back wall. It was like excavating a Pharaoh's tomb in Egypt, it must be a good few years since anyone had been in here. To our amazement and great amusement, there was behind the door, the holy grail to a group of mid pubescent young boys, a sanitary towel dispenser, how cool!

We managed to get one out, hiding it quickly in a pocket like it was fags or drugs. When break came we showed it to our mates, giving them a quick glance beneath a coat as if we were selling guns in an Irish pub. It was funny to us but what were we going to do with it? We pondered, then after a few seconds, the three of us looked at each other and as one said, 'Mrs Jupiter'.

Mrs Jupiter was a new RE teacher of all things, she didn't seem overtly religious and if anything tried a bit too hard to be a cool friend to the kids. She was a bit wacky, and we thought someone who could take a joke. One wet playtime, when everyone was just dossing about in classrooms and corridors, she told us about the girly magazines she finds under her husband's side of the bed and how rude the stories were. Not the everyday topic for your usual Religious Education teacher. One story was about a swingers party where all the blokes started playing 'Soggy Biscuit'. We looked at her confused and innocent as she then educated us as to what happens. When you hear these words coming from the mouth of your RE teacher, you think she'd be up for a laugh!

We sneaked into the Art room, Mr Sanders who was from Sheffield and knew Joe Cocker was in the store cupboard having one of his fags. We went to the inks and dropped some 'Period Red' on the sanitary towel.
'That looks real right?' We asked each other.
Then it was on to Jupiter's room, she was marking books when we went in, we were either side of her throwing the jam rag back and forth to each other, with her playing all bothered and squealing in the middle. Then like a bad nightmare we were gone. We ran round a couple of corners outside and stopped to catch our breath, pissing ourselves laughing at how funny we were. We'd better get rid of it, where was it?
'I put it down the back of her neck!' Iggy said,
'Shit!' Now she had the evidence.

Our punishment was quite tame really, just to say prayers in front of the school assembly and quite a few detentions. But after the next parents evening, Mr Epilepsy told Mum that he had not taken the situation as far as it warranted and that we should have been expelled or at least suspended. As soon as the fake blood became part of the equation it was, in the schools eyes, assault. We did our time and in our defence, never mentioned that she had told us her 'Soggy Biscuit' story, we weren't grasses. I think she got away with more than we ever did

Academically, I did OK at school, Maths and Art were my favourite subjects, preparing me for a bright future of painting with numbers.

Science was interesting and good fun, being in the Chemistry labs with the high benches and gas taps. We were brilliant at fire breathing, filling our mouths as full as we'd dare from the little gas taps, then blowing it out into the Bunsen Burner flame of the group next to you. That burnt with a bright orange flame.

On one occasion we were being very careful, we'd just seen the teacher put a tiny piece of Sodium in water and it properly exploded, making us all jump. Having experienced the power of chemicals in such a way, we were extra cautious dealing with some petroleum derivative or bi product, I'm sure it was called Hexane? For some reason we were wearing gloves, holding the Hexane in a little metal dish using tongs, heating it above a Bunsen Burner. Before we could write down our findings, Mark Hawkins our class maths genius, started screaming in the corner like a little girl. We all looked round to see that the silly twat had set his sleeve alight. He was screaming and flapping his arms like a baby bird, he ran between the desks towards the sinks in the corner. As he passed, people were flicking their little Hexane dishes at him and by the time he reached the teacher, his arm and back were fully alight!

He was absolutely fine, the teacher pulled a fire blanket from the wall, rugby tackled him to the floor and rolled him around like a fine cigar on a Cuban virgins thigh. Someone shouted, 'Sir! Shall we write down that Mark burns with a blue flame?'

Geography was a neither here nor there subject, I quite liked it but all I seem to have retained is how an Ox-Bow lake is formed and that Cirrus clouds are wispy.

English was just an excuse to do the slow hand-clap and make the teacher cry.

French I liked, we always went to France as a family on holiday and Dad was a fluent speaker. As a kid he used to spend whole holidays there with his student exchange family, people used to ask what part of Paris he was from, his accent was that good. We were blessed with a French student teacher for a couple of terms called Fabienne, she was a stunner. She took us for French Aural where we all sat in a big circle, all the boys rushing to get the seat next to her. I buggered up my French Aural exam when trying to answer,
'What do I like to do at the weekend?'
Evidently I said,
'I like to play Pool in the Brothel,' instead of Public House.

My biggest exam disappointment of all was Technical Drawing. I'd sailed through the mock exams and the teacher had put me down as an expected Grade A. He was the toughest teacher in the school and no one mucked about when in 'The Hitch's' class. He stressed all the time how important the accuracy and cleanliness of your work was. I liked that, marks were lost when grubby finger prints or smudges appeared and we were always washing our hands, to keep our work pristine.

I was about 20 minutes away from the end of the exam, very pleased with my helix, nice crisp lines and not a mark on the sheet that shouldn't be there. All of a sudden, while congratulating myself and basking in my magnificence, a 2p sized red splat appeared on my work, then another, then a third. Bloody nosebleed! I pulled my head back and the blood streamed across my sheet and onto the drawing board. It looked like a scene from a Tarantino movie, my work was ruined. I was hoping that extenuating circumstances might be taken into account, but in the end I got a D.

I really enjoyed sport at school, I was one of the tallest in the year so had I had an unfair advantage at some of the athletic events. Cricket never interested me, we used to stand in the outfield and see how many laps of the pitch we could do, before the teacher noticed.

If you were good at sport you got a lot easier time from the teachers. One of them was a hard bastard, he came from the army and shouted at us like we were his little squaddies. The chubby, middle aged head of department was a bit easier on the ear, but did have some funny hygiene rules.

At our first ever lesson in Year 1 he told us that we mustn't wear pants under our shorts, just the shorts. He said that it was unhygienic, to get all sweaty playing football then sit in our next lesson with sweaty pants on, so we had to go commando.

He also insisted everyone shower properly after sport, so much so, that he used to stand at the shower entrance to make sure we were soaping ourselves up properly. I think it was in the third year, we were in the middle of winter and the snow was a foot deep and crisp and even around the school. The girls had taken over the sports hall and gym, so we all went to a classroom and watched a technical video about how to throw a rugby ball. We were all in our uniforms but he still made us have a shower afterwards. He left the school soon after that.

My favourite Sports teacher was also my Maths teacher, I passed my Maths O'level a year early and also took Statistics, so I was off to a favourable start. He had spent time in America and was really good at and pushed Basketball as a sport. It wasn't that popular in schools back then. I managed to get into the County Basketball team at their trials, the only person from our school, so he loved me for that too.

My first game for the County was away to Hertfordshire, the venue was a Catholic school in St. Albans. Only a few of us, who were at the same schools, knew each other so there wasn't much af a team spirit or camaraderie. When we had changed and entered the court, everyone trying to hide their nerves, we watched them warming up. We didn't stand a chance in Hell. They were all over six foot and looked like the Harlem Globetrotters, flicking the ball between them like a hot potato. I gave a good account of myself and was our highest scorer with 18 points. We only lost 186-30.

What I thought could be a promising sporting career, took another blow shortly after. The teachers across the country were having a pay dispute and as one, stopped doing extra curricular activities, so even though my first game for my County was also my last, I was the County's top scorer that year.

One of our good friends that played in the school basketball team was Zed, he was one of the gang. Zed was of Greek Cypriot descent and still had grandparents on the island. He had a facial deformity but as he'd been one of our mates for years we didn't give it a second thought. He suffered from Rhino something or other, a deformation of the nose, everything else was normal but for all intent and purposes, he was basically born with an upside down nose.

It was a couple of years after we'd all left school that we heard Zed had died. He was holidaying with his parents and grandparents in Cyprus, when he got caught out by a really severe Mediterranean storm. There was really bad torrential rain, a months worth in one day, he'd forgotten his special rain hat and drowned as he ran to safety from the beach.
Zeds Dead baby, Zeds Dead, very sad.

4 College

After leaving school I was accepted into Suffolk Art College in Ipswich, it was a two year foundation course, a Lower Diploma for artistic types. The course gave you the chance to try all aspects of arts and crafts and then decide what you wanted to specialise in for a Higher Diploma.

The more arty creatives favoured subjects like Ceramics, Fine Art, Art History and Jewellery Making. I was more interested in Graphics, Typography, Photography and Printing, although the former were great fun to try.

Every minute of the two years were like being in a grown-up youth club, it was nothing like school. It was so relaxed, you could drink, smoke and wear what you liked, the main plus was that I was interested in all the subjects.

The tutors were a waste of space, all of them failed artists who'd been stoned since the 60s. They spent less time teaching than trying to be cool. They tried to be trendy like the young adults we were, while still listening to Santana and the Grateful Dead and wearing brown corduroy.

The social life was great, to their credit the tutors spent the first few weeks getting to know the students by taking them round all the pubs near the college and docks. Then, at no particular time, it was back to lessons to draw some shit.

One example of the 'shit' we had to draw, was when we were told to make a great mountain of bent wood chairs, not stacked neatly, just a big mess of chairs about 10ft high.
Jan the Pole prepared us,
'Right guys you all see the chairs yeah? I don't want you to draw the chairs but draw the spaces between the chairs, the negative space. Or if you'd rather, make a mark showing how you think those voids are feeling'.
What a Grade 1 Knobhead.

When we were told we'd be doing life drawing we couldn't wait, this was one of the reasons, that the boys at least, had chosen Art College. Until that was, we saw Ethel the model, not pleasing on the eyes and the wrong side of 60. She had definately fallen out of the ugly tree as a baby and hit every branch on the way down. She was standing outside the portakabin in a dressing gown having a smoke. We all filed past her up the steps, while she finished her fag, shivering and stomping her feet.

We sat in a big circle with drawing boards on our laps, waiting for her to drape herself around the dirty old chez long in the middle. This was the first time we'd had Ethel posing and it was only when she started pouring her ample self out of the dressing gown, that I realised the mistake I'd made.

I was sat at the foot end of the chez, and as such, had the lions share of her podgy snatch staring back at me. I could have sworn it winked at me, from under its matted mono-brow of wispy, old lady hair. As the portakabin was a bit draughty, there were three fan heaters all aimed at the Ethel. It was like a sauna in there, the riverlets of sweat started to appear like little mountain springs, winding their random journey down her body to pool in the lucky material she lay on. With the smell of sweat and the oppressive heat, the only thing hard in the room, was to do a decent drawing.

Jewellery was a really interesting subject, it was never going to be my career choice but it was good to be creative and actually make something tangible. If we made something out of silver or gold, we'd get the raw materials at a heavily subsidised price. We ended up making the most ridiculous, un-wearable massive rings out of the thickest gauge of silver we could, the college would weigh the finished item and charge us three or four quid.
Then at lunch we were straight down to the jewellers in town, next to the Town Hall, opposite the pub, who'd weigh it again and give us the going rate for silver, tripling our money.

My favourite subject I think was Photography, with all the freedom it gave us. The teacher actually knew his stuff and Nick Kershaw was an ex pupil, so he was a good teacher and also had Pop Star stories.

The Photography annex was on the other side of town, we'd go in first thing to pick up a camera and load it with film, remember film? Once armed with our cameras, we were told to go off and photograph things.

If it was raining we usually went to Ipswich Museum next door, they had a stuffed Giraffe and reconstructions of Mediaeval villages, in a lovely Victorian building. That was until pub o'clock when we'd go down the hill into town and do photographic studies of Pub Culture, its patrons and the pub's effect on society. If you ever went to the toilets without your camera, when developing the film later you'd usually find a random knob, nipple of tit pic.

On a nice day my mate Adrian and myself, might take some cans to the park and do a photographic study of Park Culture, its people and the sun's effect on society.

Our favourite subject matter by far was 'Fuck Off', an old man with Mother Theresa's face, one tooth and a dog wrapped in newspaper on a piece of string. He shuffled the streets of Ipswich rain or shine, slowly sanding the soles of his shoes away against the pavement, shouting at everyone to 'Fuck Off!' We'd follow him slowly, then rush ahead hiding in a doorway, waiting for the perfect shot, like trainee paparazzi stalking the easiest prey.

On one occasion we had been following him a while, he gradually slowed his shuffle, shouted 'FUCK!' and his feet completely stopped, we looked at each other and went closer, he'd actually fallen asleep walking. Standing in the middle of the pavement, mid 'Fuck Off!' His dog just sitting at his feet. We went as close as we dare, taking some great pictures, then suddenly he straightened bolt upright and shouted 'OFF!' And resumed his shuffle again, What a character.

It was a long time ago and my memories of Art College, are like fingerprints on an abandoned handrail, but there were quite a few characters from Ipswich, that I can remember, a real cross-section of society.

Adrian was a close friend, he was hating the late 80s because the Americans and monkeys had just invented the disease AIDS, obviously that was going to be his nickname for the duration.

There were a couple of middle aged mums who'd kids had left home and were obviously passing the menopause years by going back to school. At least they had each other to talk to. A girl called Tertia, the third born daughter and a long haired blond called Mary-Jane who didn't realise she was named after drugs.

The biggest character by far was Pirate Pete, a really genuine funny guy. A few years before college, he'd been playing football

on a Saturday, after the match his foot started aching. His
mum was a nurse and said that he'd probably done his boots
up too tight. He had a game on the Sunday and had to go off
in the second half. That evening his foot started swelling up
and smelling funny. He had to be rushed to hospital and that
evening had his foot amputated. The morning after they cut his
leg off just below the knee and two days later just below his hip,
leaving him about an eight inch stump. A sobering thought for
us all, he was playing football on the Sunday and by Wednesday
only had one leg!

Pete was amazing the way he dealt with his situation, admittedly
he smoked way too much weed, but who wouldn't if they were
in his shoe? He quite openly talked about his leg and his Bionics,
it wasn't a subject we had to pussy foot around. His bionic leg
was amazing, a symphony of titanium, springs and pistons,
when he had it on under jeans you couldn't tell it was fake, he
didn't even have a limp.

He had a very pretty girlfriend he'd known for years, we asked
if there were any awkward moments when they shagged for the
first time, he said he couldn't remember any, then added,
'The thing is, when you've only got one leg, you can really get
right up there! She loves it!'

Quite often he wouldn't bother with the prosthetic leg but
use his crutches, we didn't like this, purely because his stride
on crutches was a couple of feet longer than ours, he would
casually stroll down the High Street and we'd all be jogging next
to him, we couldn't keep up.

In the winter he'd wear a long grey coat with a stuffed parrot
sewn onto the shoulder. At Christmas time he would wear a
pair of convertible trousers with detachable legs. He'd sit down
in the pub, unzip the right trouser leg, revealing his bionic leg
entwined with Christmas fairy lights. We'd plug him in and he'd

sit there like a Christmas tree in the corner, we had to get his drinks all night once he was plugged in!

Another good friend was Fung, he was my snooker buddy, he was a couple of years older than me, having chosen to do A'levels before college. His parents, who lived in Hong Kong, owned a restaurant and he lived with his Nan and Sister near Ipswich Airport.

It was great learning about his different culture, he taught me one to ten in Chinese and how to say 'I've got a yellow car,' it was all I could think that I wanted to say in Chinese. Looking back on it, if I ever did go to Hong Kong I wouldn't have my car with me, so it was probably a waste of time learning it.

Fung's nan was a hoot, she had lived in England for years yet her English stretched to 'Hello', she was always welcoming and still chatted to me knowing I hadn't a clue what she was on about.

Once Fung was without a car and asked me if I would drive his Nan to the dentist, he told me the deatils, I said no problem if he OK'd it with Fat John the tutor first. I followed him, like a lamb to the slaughter, here was little Chinese Fung having to ask for permission to take his even smaller Chinese Nan to the dentist at half past two. Fat John told him to Piss Off, not wanting to be the but of a joke that wasn't there, after five minutes of explaining the tooth hurty joke to Fung, still not really believing him, he gave his permission.

Another character was Fung's auntie, she owned a fish and chip shop near the college and we used to visit once a week on a Friday for a chippy lunch. One busy day we were behind a gaggle of school kids and immediately behind a very American couple of tourists reading a guide book.

When the Americans came to order they took ages.

'Hey Elinor ya want some Cod fish?'

'Yeah honey and fries,' she said,

'They do chips, they're like big fries,' he said, 'You want?'

'Yeah honey.' Elinor replied,

He ordered with his eyes not moving from the board on the wall,

'Can I get one Cod Fish and a helping of your large Chips,
then can I get another Cod Fish and one Sausage in Batter and
another portion of Chips. No wait, hold the Sausage in Batter,
I'll just have the Cod Fish and a portion of Chips.'

Fung's auntie wrapped their order, put it down on the counter
and firmly said,

'Cod and Chips Twice!' They walked out the shop and she looked
at us, tutted and said, 'Broody Foreigners!'

The one thing Fung surprisinly wasn't into was gambling, he
never went on the fruit machine and showed little interest of
going to a casino. Not wanting to stereotype him, but I thought
gambling was part of Chinese culture, like tasty food, tasty ladies
and living to over 100.

Fung had a nice XR3i, not bad car for a 21 year old Art Student,
it put my 10 year old Polo to shame. One day he said out of the
blue, "We're going shopping, I want to get another car."

His dad had cleaned up at the Punto Banco table back home and
wired him six grand, we looked around 'Motor City' near the
Airport for a couple of lunchtimes and he ended up getting a
slightly newer XR3i, now he had two.

It was less than a month before his dad called and said he had
to sell both cars and send him back the money, this time he'd
lost the restaurant in a dice game and needed the cash to win it
back. This evidently was a common occurrence and within the
next month his dad won his restaurant back and sent enough for
another car, I can see why Fung didn't partake.

5 Colchester

After two years in Ipswich it was time for me for me to grow up, to cut the apron strings and move away from the family home. I loved Mum and Dad, having my washing done and meals cooked for me, but I was 18 and it was time for proper independence. No more would I live in the middle of a field in Suffolk, I had the whole country to choose from and I was in charge of my destiny.

My main college choices were Lincoln and Bournemouth, both far away enough for a new start, new people, my own house and a new way of life. When we went to see the colleges and what they had to offer, I made a point of buying local newspapers and leaflets from Tourist Information to educate myself about the areas. These were after all, places I'd never been, I read up about local attractions and places to go. I'd spend hours scanning through the property and rooms to let sections, building my potential future life in my head. The excitement was unbearable.

In the end I got accepted in Colchester, 10 miles from Mum and Dad's house and closer to home now, than when I was in Ipswich. I'd be staying with Nanny Car's friend Sue, who had two spare bedrooms. A drinking buddy from Ipswich, Em took the other room and we soon got to know everyone, finding out who on the course lived near us.

Moz was a Brummy, he came from Ironbridge and had the strongest Midlands accent I'd ever tried to understand. Despite his accent was very intelligent and had 12 O'levels. He supported Villa with a passion and played occasionally for FA Cup giant killers Telford FC, 'The Lilywhites' like the tampon. We spent most evenings and weekends in the Sun Inn then finished up at his digs, he shared with two others and they had a three bedroom, proper grown up house all to themselves.

They had free run of the whole house and its garden, the only bit out of bounds was the mysterious padlocked loft. Their landlord was a big black American bloke, he was ex army and Moz said really easy going, as we later found out when opening the loft, he collected magazines with naked oiled up men straddling motorbikes and lifting hay bales. Moz only saw him a couple of times that year and each time he'd halved in weight, we thought either he had the big disease with a little name or he was a method actor like Tom Hanks in Philadelphia.

Mongo was another character, he was an Indian lad from Huddersfield, always trying to duck and dive with his money making schemes. We voted him the most likely in the year to either become a millionaire or end up in prison, to this day I don't know which he achieved. He came from quite a strict religious family and was really making the most of his freedom, but as any college breaks approached he'd grow a full beard to go home with. His Dad had several businesses in Yorkshire, restaurants, newsagents and a taxi firm. On more than one occasion he'd come back to college driving a nice Mercedes to sell down South, one of his dad's taxis, they sold for more near London than in Yorkshire evidently.

One such time, Mongo took Geordie and I on a trip to
test drive a Porsche. We have a collection of dealerships in
Colchester, Ferrari and Porsche being next to each other.
Mongo thought we looked too young to be potential Ferrari
drivers so we pulled up to the Porsche garage in his Dad's
E-Class. The story was that we ran a top Design Agency and
had been doing so well that he wanted to treat himself to a nice
company car and would put the Mercedes up in part exchange.
You could smell the bullshit as soon as Mongo opened his
mouth and I'm sure the salesman was just humouring us. To
be fair though we did get a ride in a 924, Geordie and me both
over six foot, squashed into the back of the 2+2, nearly on each
others laps. Mongo sailed down the A12 at 80-90mph, ignoring
the salesman every time he suggested to come off at a junction
so we could head back.

Mongo got away with many a misdemeanor in the two years
we were all together, until the very last day. Everyone was
celebrating at the Marquis, the closest pub to college and our
regular watering hole. Moz and myself left the celebrations
to rejoin later that evening. We had to go back to the empty
college to get the last of our things, we approached the stairwell,
opened the doors and could hear Mongo's bullshit flowing
down the steps. He was standing there with an accomplice, half
way down the stairs holding an A0 drawing board and stand he
was trying to steal, discussing his actions with the principal.

We got our stuff and waited outside to see what was going to
happen, expecting the police to drive up and take Mongo. When
he emerged with his usual big grin, he told us that he was free
to go, he quoted the Principal saying, that he knew he'd stolen
so much college stuff over the past two years and was just so
happy that he'd finally caught him doing something.

When settling in to Colchester college life weekends were usually filled with pub crawls around town, each pub had its own character and establishments were chosen depending on whether the girls were coming out or not.

Me and Moz would wet our whistles in our local Sun Inn then catch the bus into town. Getting off in the High Street we'd go straight to The Lamb, you had to go here early and sober or the pick pockets at the door would clean you out before you even got to the bar. We'd get our pints and sit behind them watching their moves as we waited for the others.

As you entered the pub there was a low brick wall to the right of the door, where Mr Sticky Fingers would sit. As the victims walked in they naturally turn to the left, to go to the bar. At this point Mr Sticky had the wallet from their back pocket and put his hand behind him, where a girl would take it and walk to the bar, before she got there she passed it to another who took it up stairs to the mezzanine. Within 10 seconds the wallet was empty and half a pub away, before the poor sod at the bar had ordered his drinks.

Colchester being a garrison town obviously had to provide watering holes for the squaddie killing machines being trained, meaning that The Bull and Coach and Horses were out of bounds to us, if there was any aggro I don't think half a dozen Art Students would last too long. They had a reputation for starting excitement, throwing stun grenades around and letting off smoke canisters. The worst we ever did was blowing up condoms on our heads.

There was one tiny little pub, next to the cinema, that the straight from school squaddies went to, they were only 16 or 17, just left school or borstal and yet to be taught how to kill a man. If they ever got asked for ID and weren't served, we thought it was funny that they're old enough to be handed a gun to kill but not a pint of beer to drink. They were all up for a bit of banta and if any did get too confrontational, you just led them outside knowing that the Military Police cars did loops of the town, as soon as they were spotted the cocksure squaddie would disappear, leaving just the smell of him shitting himself.

On a couple of occasions my little brother Pip and his mate Handbrake came out with us, both of them 17 stones of muscle, Pip was six feet tall, built like the Terminator and wore his biker jacket, Handbrake was smaller and rounder but just as deadly. He was once cutting wood with a circular saw, hit a nail and the saw bounced back slicing a three inch deep wound in his belly, he only needed stitches because it hadn't gone deep enough to reach any of his vital organs. They both had shaved heads with soap spiked crowns at the front, and leave me alone faces.

In those days I always struggled with reverse parking, especially with six people in my little car, when I had these two with me, I just had to reverse at an vague angle, Pip and Handbrake would get out and lift the front of the car and engine nearer the kerb.

One time we decided to go into the Coach and Horses, the no-go killer squaddie pub, it was only early and the atmosphere hadn't turned bad yet. We'd been in there an hour or so, Me, Moz, Geordie and Handbrake were having a drink in the corner and Pip had gone for a piss. He came out five minutes later with the condom machine under his arm, put it down on the bar, and started moaning at the barman that it had swallowed his 50p. As the barman explained, he could have just told him and not taken it off the wall, we quickly grabbed Pip and left apologising as we went.

Minty one of our classmates, worked as barman in a pub near the town station, this was handy if we were a bit short and needed some beer credit. It was also the only pub I've ever seen with a 20ft well in the basement. Minty brought it to our attention because he'd just split up with his girlfriend, and evidently the well was a famous place for getting your own back on ex girlfriends or boyfriends. His ex was a music student at college, they had the block next to our art department and we shared the coffee room. She was gorgeous, a blond Cellist that obviously had trouble keeping her knees together after she'd stopped playing, she had started blowing a flautist from the year above. Minty had some dirty Polaroids of her because phone cameras hadn't been invented yet. We went over to the well, the bricks were waist high and there was an iron grid over the top, looking down you could see that hundreds of compromising photos had been pushed through the grid and now lay at the bottom, with quite a few landing facing up. One by one he pushed his little squares of revenge through the grate, over half landing good side up. I asked,

'Is that better now? You got closure?'

'Yeah, Slag,' he said, 'Who wants a drink?'

One Saturday I was at a loose end, all the boys had gone home for the weekend and Moz had been called up to play for Telford, he got his travel paid for and £25 match fee so couldn't turn it down.

I was walking into town near the station when a bloke approached me from the road, I looked round and noticed he'd just got off the first of two coaches that had pulled up. He asked for directions to Layer Road, the then home of Colchester United. Both coaches were full of Wolves fans, I looked at my watch, it was getting very close to kick off and they're still a way from the ground.

I walked over to the coach so that the driver could hear my directions too and I told them where they'd gone wrong.

They'd left the A12 one junction too soon and as the football ground was right next to Colchester Zoo, they should get back on the A12, take next exit and follow the brown signs with the elephant on to the Zoo. Once at the Zoo they'd see the stadium next to it.

They thanked me and hurried back on-board, beeping as they left, I acknowledged their beep with a raised arm and watched as they chugged off in the direction of the main road.

All afternoon I was wondering when they had realised the Zoo was nowhere near the football ground. Did they just say sod it, call me a wanker and have a wander around the Zoo, or did they ask someone else and try to make the second half.

One of any young man's most life changing moments is when you are finally united with your true love, your life partner. The one thing that finally proves you've grown up, you forsake all others, forget all the outlandish dreams, the would and could have beens and settle for what God has betrothed to you. You can take her whenever you want, never again having to ask permission, you can travel the world together and your names are together on that little piece of paper that legally confirms your ownership.

My first car was a 1978 Riyad Yellow VW Polo, only 895cc but that wasn't a gauge to the fun it gave, just how slowly it gave it. It had been bought new as our family car over 10 years previously, amassing over 100,000 miles and while I was just borrowing it here and there previously, I had dinged nearly every panel and I think mum just didn't want to be seen in it anymore.

Mum and Dad had plans on a new car and the condition I had put the Polo in had reduced its trade-in value so much, that they might as well just give it to me. This was two years into college, the perfect time to have the freedom of the roads and say goodbye to bus travel forever.

One thing I realised for the first time being a car owner, was that you have to accept responsibility for your actions, if you hit someone you have to stop and give your details, usually to a proper grown up whose day you've ruined and who never really wants to just laugh about it.

One freezing mid winter day I had stopped at some traffic lights on a slight hill approaching Colchester High Street. There was a little, ancient, hat and coated lady with a tartan push along shopper 20-30ft from me, looking very unsure as whether to start crossing or stay and wait. She looked like a revving car with the handbrake on, lurching to go then changing her mind. She'd gone through the end of a red man, through the green man now red man again. My lights were now green and I edged forward still unsure of her plans, as soon as I moved she went for it, two tiny biddy steps into the road, I slammed on the brakes, the wheels locked on the greasy road but still stopping a good 20ft away from her, as I stopped she looked at me with her arms and legs in a frightened spasm, eyes staring like the proverbial rabbit, then she sort of crumpled herself to the road with a yelp.

Just as I was thinking 'Ah bless, she's too old to be out alone,' I could feel the whole street looking at me, I could see an old lady that had fallen over 20ft away, they were seeing a student in a car that must have been going too fast, because the woman he'd hit had flown 20ft though the air landing in a crumpled heap.

I pulled to the side as the Samaritans helped her to vertical,
'She all right?' I asked,
'You shouldn't been going that fast!' One twat shouted at me.
'You have to give your details!' He said.
I went up to him and told him nicely that I had fucking stopped when she fell over, and all I had done was not drive over an old lady that was laying in the fucking road.

'You didn't even see anything happen so be quiet.' She was fine, so I drove back to college, well the police never came to find me so she must have been OK.

My newly found mobility pushed the boundaries of how far we could now travel come the weekend, no longer were we tethered to the High Street, football or the local, the world was our oyster. One weekend we went to a car show in Chelmsford. Me, Moz and girlfriends in tow, we saw all the customised cars, filling my head full of ideas for my Polo.

Toilet time for the lads was easy, we could just piss against the tree with a beach windbreak around it, 20 seconds later we're all done. The girls though had a queue of at least 50 desperadoes in a line facing a portakabin. We decided to be gentlemen and queue with them.

The portakabin we learnt, as we watched the system, had a woman in charge who opened the front door, inside were five cubicles with no doors facing the front. When all five had shaken the lettuce and were done a side door was opened by another attendant for their exit, then five more went into the front again. Like the Falkland jets, we counted them out and we counted them in again. Until, that is, we were getting close to the front and noticed that five had gone in but only four came out, the front door was opened leaving one poor cow squatting, just finishing off in the cubicle directly facing the queue, frozen, she didn't know whether to finish wiping or just pull her knickers up and run. I'm sure it felt like ages to her but the door lady soon shut off the view and the poor cow flew out the side disappearing into the crowd, I hope it wasn't a poo.

6 London

After college I decided that London was the place to be, so I loaded my little Polo with all my worldly possessions, clothes, music and portable battery TV/Cassette/Radio. I figured that it would save on travelling time and petrol money actually being based in London, and surely it would only take a week or so to find a house share or room somewhere.

My home was a car park on the edge of a bit of green open space, just off the Edgware Road in North West London. It was just round the corner from my girlfriends parents house where I was allowed to wash when they'd gone out.

It was while I was spending a lot of time alone in my Polo in London that I had quite a few inspirational inventions pop into my head, I had a large sketch pad and my ideas flowed like a towns traffic in a well planned one-way system.

My best ideas were inspired by an ex who loved horse riding, she couldn't, or wouldn't, explain to me why it was so enjoyable, in my mind it was obviously a sexual thing and the constant rocking motion of the horse, must provided the same pleasure to a lady that a washing machine on spin does, but in a field or country lane setting.

My invention was the Dil-Daddle, it looked like a normal saddle but there was a lever you could slide, this engorged a soft leather dildo to enhance the riding experience if needed. Not forgetting the cowboys, there was another version for them, the Vaga-Daddle, again looking like a standard saddle but with a sliding leather cover that, when opened, revealed a self lubricating vagina shaped pocket for nobby to go in, made from the softest chamois leather, I'm sure cowboys must get a bit bone willy while riding too.

Argos had a brilliant 16 day returns policy, so I bought a battery powered electric travel razor for £15.99. It was only a stop gap to use while in my car, I obviously had nowhere to plug my mains razor so I used it for two weeks, cleaned it very well, returned it, got my money back and bought another one, like a razor rental.

It was a cosy little set up, I had a private car park overlooking a nice little bit of heathland, the back seats folded flat providing a surprisingly comfortable bed when under my nice warm duvet. I had the little 5" black and white TV to watch on my 'Entertainment Centre' until the batteries died and my girlfriend provided coffee, and a hot bacon and tommy sarnie every morning.

One evening we decided to go to the cinema on Edgware Road, it was a week night and the cinema had a quiet, rough, pot-holed area just behind it to park in. The film was OK, Beetlejuice I think, but when we got back to the car I noticed that the drivers side little quarter light had been smashed. My car had been broken into!

Thieving bastards! They'd had obviously seen that there was a quantity of stuff in the back, even though I'd covered it with my duvet. I was gutted, everything I had was in there and some dirty London scum thought he could just help himself.

I checked in the passenger foot well and my TV was still there, thank God, the car radio was there, all my tapes were in the front door pocket, they'd been rifled through but nothing missing. Maybe they didn't like Alien Sex Fiend, The Birthday Party and Scraping Foetus off the Wheel, everyone's a critic! All of my clothes were there and it seems nothing was taken. Not only had some little wanker smashed my window, but he'd also told me that all my stuff was shit and I own nothing worth taking.

I felt violated and dirty. I assessed the situation and thought I wouldn't be able to leave an open car in London, maybe the next person to have a look might be a really desperate homeless, who'd at least have the decency to take something. I covered up the broken window with cardboard and rape tape, ready for the drive home, at least we didn't have car crime in Suffolk.

Once home, I spent a couple of days realising how comfortable a real bed was and what a shit-hole London was. It wasn't even approaching a nice place to be so I'd look for a job a bit closer to home.

7 Freedom

Life after college was exciting, we were set free into the real world like pigeons of promise, a world with no rules and my only timetable was self imposed, it was; Get up - Make Mum and Dad proud - Go to bed.

My mates Moz, Mongo, Geordie, Fingering Frank from the Hoe, Dirty Di and Steph had all sodded off to their respective parts of the country, to fulfil their dreams. I was living with Scouse, he had another year at Art College after the summer break and was staying in town. He'd found digs in a small Victorian terraced house in not a great area, but very handy if you needed a tattoo, kebab or a hangover.

As with anyone from Liverpool, you have to ask if the have any Beatles anecdotes. One of my mum's friends has a big photo of her and a friend together with John Lennon and Paul McCartney back in the 60s, and she didn't even come from Liverpool.

I did ask Scouse but he had no Beatles stories. He said that most of the stories weren't true anyway and that if everyone who said they'd seen the Beatles in the Cavern Club, had actually been

there, it would have to be the size of Wembley Stadium. I was a
bit disappointed but he paused for a few seconds, had a sip of
his pint, then revealed,
'My Grandad did go to Art College with Hitler though! And his
Dad lived next door to Hitler's brother in Toxteth!'
I thought, that beats any Beatles story I'd ever heard hands
down and I bought Scouse another pint.

Scouse had a spare room in his digs and his landlady never
checked up on him, she just popped in to get his rent once a
week. He left her cash in an envelope in the sideboard drawer
that his telly sat on, next to his guitar and just before the
kitchen, she knew it was there for her if he was ever out.

The landlady Sonia, would have been a MILF Scouse said but
she didn't have any children. She had never met me and didn't
know I was squatting but she did know of my interest in her
vacant room.

One Saturday morning I was alone in the house watching The
Banana Splits and waiting for the Monkees to come on, when
someone knocked on the front door. I stayed where I was,
couldn't be bothered to get up, a key turned in the lock and
I froze as the landladies boyfriend let himself in. Scouse had
never met him but said he was a local Radio DJ, and that he had
been described as looking like Mr T!

He seemed very pleasant, dripping in gold and speaking with a
velvety, midnight Jazz Radio voice, I turned the sound down on
the TV as he walked over to me, hand out for a shake, and said,
'Allirght mate, you must be Scouse?'
Shit, I wasn't supposed to be there, what was I to do?
So obviously, I greeted him in my best Liverpool accent.
'Ahhlight Laa, You must be Bruno!'
I thought I sounded great!
I went to the drawer and got the envelope out, how could I not

be Scouse? He thanked me and soon left, I must have
been convincing.

I did formally meet Sonia a couple of days later and she did
query whether it was me that met Bruno, it must have been
because I was a lot taller than Scouse, I know my accent was
spot on.

I really needed a job, passing the time was fine and I could now
play five chords on the guitar, the intro to Smokestack Lightnin'
and The Wind Cries Mary but that wasn't going to butter
many parsnips!

Design Week magazine was the place to find jobs, obviously
most of them were in London but I did find an advert for
Junior Designer in Oxford, a nice place I thought, maybe
a change of scene would do me good. I got invited to an
interview, loaded up my little yellow Polo with my portfolio,
cans of coke and snacks for the journey and set off for Oxford,
it was miles away from Colchester, a proper test for my little car.

Arriving in Oxford, it seemed extremely clean with very little
traffic, more like a Town than a City and not at all threatening
like London. I remember going past their football ground and
I could tell that I was approaching the more salubrious side of
town, as peoples front doors got further and further from the
pavement. I turned into a very well to do Avenue, there were
enormous family homes either side and eventually an imposing
10ft high, red brick wall on the right, this is what I was looking
for and that was my cue to indicate.

I drove between the impressive iron gates and was greeted by
around 50 chanting picketers, standing around a couple of bins
on fire. It was a proper donkey-jacketed union picket line, like
you see up north on't telly. I knew the job had something to do
with Robert Maxwell, so I assumed I must be in the right place.
The comrade that greeted me was surprisingly affable, he told

me where to park and where reception was, the crowd didn't shout Scab or throw anything at me as I drove through.

The house was gigantic, resembling a Stately Home, maybe it was Maxwell's actual house? The car park was away to the right, the deep gravel drive winding its way between specimen Cedar and Oak trees to a wooded area.
I found a space away from other cars and parked up. I had over an hour until the interview and was bursting for a piss, I got out and stretched my legs, God it had been a long drive, I was 123 miles away from home cooking.

Looking around there wasn't a sole, I skipped over a large log and found the perfect private piss place, about 3 trees away from the car. The stream only just waited for my zip to open and splashed violently against the giant firs bark. I stepped back and continued the flow, first arcing from side to side then up and down, still going, the best pisses are always the urgent pisses I thought. It must have been over 30 seconds before the torrent slowed and dribbled its finale. I checked my flies were locked, hair in the car window and waited for my time to shine.

The interviewer was a nice lady, quite young, she explained that the job involved mainly designing a newsletter for Czechoslovakian immigrants. I think I made all the right noises, stopping just short of saying that I'd always wanted to work on newsletters for Czechoslovakian immigrants.
I asked pertinent questions and felt that I'd given a good representation of myself. I shook her hand goodbye and it was only as I passed reception again, that I noticed my car on one of the surveillance screens behind the desk. Oh look there was another screen with my car in the distance, the camera aimed straight at my perfect private piss place tree! I didn't get that job but spotted the camera attached to a tree when I got back to the car.

One interview that didn't go that well was for a highly respected Design company in Barnes, a really pricey part of London just south of the river.

Again I arrived in plenty of time and luckily found a space on the road right outside the company, even better there was a pub right next door. As I had a couple of hours to kill I went into the pub, had a very agreeable if not too expensive, Ham and Cheese Toasty with Chips. Obviously just a Coke to drink and so as not to look like a Billy no-mates, alone on a table for one, I changed a fiver into coins for the fruity.

Still in plenty of time, I had a wee and left the pub to get my portfolio from the car, better to be early. After two steps along the pavement I looked up, key in hand and realised that the car had gone. I spotted a traffic warden down the road, who took great pleasure in telling me that I'd parked in a tow zone and my car was in the car pound. The car I could deal with, but my portfolio was in the back, I couldn't even attend the interview. I told the interviewer my situation and he rearranged it for the week after. It only took me three hours to get the tube to car pound, wait to be seen, phone Dad who sorted out the fine over the phone, and be on my merry way back to Colchester. I did the whole journey again the week after, parking carefully this time, but I still didn't get the job.

One job that I did get was as Night Cashier on the south bound carriageway of the A12. The hours were 10pm to 7am, Friday and Saturday, I figured this was a good idea as I'd both be earning money and captive on drinks nights, so not spending it.

The manager who saw me Paul, was no more than 25. A little bloke about 5'2" with immaculate side parted, highlighted blond hair who walked like a dancer trying to hold a poo in. As he showed me around, he reassured me that everything had

been done to make the cashier as safe as possible through the night shift.
The previous night cashier had been shot at through the bullet proof glass with a shot gun and received a few flesh wounds. The windows had now been replaced with bomb proof glass and what was a perspex lid to the cash tray was now steel, so everything is now as safe as it could be.

I was shown the ropes on my first night, by Two Meter Peter, he was a very tall 6'6" but probably only weighed about 140 pounds soaking wet. He had immaculate side parted, highlighted blond hair and he walked like a dancer trying to hold in a poo too.

Customers at first were few and far between, maybe three or four every half hour until midnight, when they seemed to completely stop. This was when I was supposed to do my chores, I had to count the fags, sandwiches, burgers and fries in the freezer and mop the shop floor. The doors front and back were locked electrically at Midnight by a switch near the till, so every transaction had to happen through the bomb proof cash tray.

I was coping OK and around half past one, Peter said he needed to see the manager, who I presumed was only still there as it was my first night.
'Just buzz the bell if you need anything!' He said.
I heard the manager's office door lock behind him, this was probably a safety thing. He was in there for over an hour, they must have had a lot to chat about.

After a couple of weekends being wet nursed by Peter and Paul, I was trusted to run the shop alone. Although they both stayed in the office until midnight for a couple of weeks, 'Chewing the Fat', probably staying on site to check I was OK. Then after they'd finished off, slid into their cars and driven away, I was in charge, Head Honcho, Numero Uno!

This was the time before CCTV had become so very popular, we had one camera aimed at the night hatch and another showing the diesel pumps for lorries, behind the shop. The first weekend had shown me that everything is dead quiet until around three in the morning, then all Hell lets loose. All the pissed people from all the clubs in Colchester were released, all of them with the bloody munchies!

That weekend I was running about like a tit in a trance, between the till and the microwave on the back wall. Every frozen Burger, Hot Dog and Chips needed heating individually for 2-3 minutes. Every number plate had to be written down, in case they drove off without paying. Everyone lifting a pump wanted okaying within seconds and everyone wanting to pay wouldn't just shut the fuck up for a minute.

When the third sluring piss-head requested four burgers and chips for his car full of piss-head mates, I knew something had to be done, I had to make an executive decision. After at least an hour of mayhem the crazy shit started to die down and I could think again. Any late stragglers wanting hot food, were now greeted with my new hand written 'OUT OF ORDER' sign, clearly visible on the front of the microwave, it worked a treat.

Our sister services over the A12 on the North bound side, used to phone for a chat now and then in the dead of night. One night in the middle of summer he called and said,
'Fancy a game of badminton?'
What a great idea. We had badminton sets in string bags outside, on top of the BBQ stuff, next to the fire logs. It was great fun, the road was so quiet, the central barrier was our net and we could get a good rally going.

You could see the headlights approaching from miles away as we were on a straight bit of road, although he soiled himself a couple of times. He had a slip road on his side about 50 meters from his forecourt with newly joining traffic, the nearest slip on my side was over half a mile away. After we'd had enough, a couple of badminton sets may have missed a shuttlecock or two, but no real harm done.

One of the perks of the job was the tips people used to leave me. When I put a customers change in the cash draw and slid the bombproof steel lid back for them to get to it, they'd quite often leave a pound coin or two in the tray for me. I'd always put their change close to them but sometimes an accidental nugget, maybe two, might roll back towards me, obscured to them by the steel lid.

These tips used to become more frequent at Club O'clock when the piss-heads arrived and they more than doubled my pay. If someone did check their change, noticing a discrepancy, I'd just tell them to check the back of the tray, saying sometimes they roll back. They'd apologise, say, 'Cheers Mate!' And be on their way.

The garage job was only ever meant to be a stop gap. My first real design job was a short stint at a Publishers in Colchester. The boss there had the habit of closing the studio every couple of years and making everyone redundant, I was there a year before he did it again.

It was a shame to have to leave, some of the titles there were right up my street. There was a Classic Car Magazine, a Paint-ball Games Magazine, a few specialist titles for Coin and Stamp Collectors and a Horse and Tack rag, for the larger bottomed riding readers.

Then came the dream job for most 21 year old single blokes like me. It was also designing magazines and also magazines that I had a passing interest in, pornography.

The job was being a designer on the best selling top shelf magazine in the country. It was 10 years after its peak in the 70s and 80s, when it sold hundreds of thousands of copies a month, 2nd only to the Radio Times in the ABC figures.

The studio was run by Moose, a mild mannered Canadian who liked snooker and his right hand man Bucko, a man you'd want in front of you in a fight. Bucko was very intelligent and very funny, but you wouldn't want to cross him. Rumour has it that none of his knuckles on his right hand lined up because, when working in the docks in Hamburg, he had a fight in a club with his own reflection, he punched a mirror because he wouldn't let himself get passed.

Then there was Timbola, a young father and the funniest man I know, he was all of the Young Ones rolled into one, except Mike the boring one! A diamond geezer from the East End, he had a dubious Uncle that used his own mum as a drugs mule.

Lastly but by no means least the biggest character of all Berger van Oepn, a Dutch South African rocker in his mid 20s. He sported shoulder length hair, snakeskin winkle pickers and shark teeth necklaces. The only person I've ever met that could walk in a room in a full-length purple velvet coat and look good, no one would bat an eyelid.

He never drank, never smoked and when asked if he was looking for drugs in Amsterdam, was quoted as saying proudly, 'Chocolate is my only Drug.'

He was a man that despite his tender years, had everything happen to him. He came out of Kings Cross tube station ten minutes before the fire that killed 31 people. He was on the plane that took off, one before a cargo flight, that crashed into flats shortly after take off from a Dutch airport killing everyone on board and over 100 people in flats on the ground.

He was once in New York, guitar on back in a bakery buying

cake. He got chatting to a 'Chick' also toting a guitar, ending up back at her apartment comparing songbooks, a thing that songwriters evidently do. She had a knock at the door and asked him to get it, standing there in front of him was Lenny Kravitz, a hero of his, Lenny just said 'Hey man, nice necklace!'

For quite a while Berger broke an unwritten rule and started 'Knowing' one of the better looking models from the magazines in a biblical way, a real no-no. She was a bit rock chic herself and eventually moved into his flat.

All of a sudden she disappeared without a trace, she'd gone leaving behind some clothes and her guitar, but not a word. Obviously there were some funny people in the porn game and we certainly came up with some crazy scenarios, but as to what happened to her, no-one knew.

Until a couple of years later, Berger found a video of her in a sex shop in Holland. She was naked on the cover, laying on a bed surrounded by six dwarfs with their six little dwarf hard-ons.

After years of telling Berger stories to others, there was always a niggling doubt that it was all completely true, could all this shit happen to just one man? About 10 years later, an old friend from the day said, 'Look at today's Sun.'

I got a copy and thumbed through, not knowing what I was looking for, until there he was, a pic of Berger van Oepn walking down a London street, being outed as part of a phone scam gang. It was a half page article and they even published his mobile number, instructing readers to call his phone, saying he's been annoying you with nuisance calls, annoy him! I checked my contacts and it was his number. The next day they published a tiny apology saying he had nothing to do with it and sorry for any distress caused. Maybe all the stories were true.

As the new boy one of my responsibilities was to pick four pictures from the reader's husbands box, this was for the page titled, 'One for the Ladies!' It was an old cardboard box that you really didn't want to put your hand in. The photos were put together in little plastic bags by Sue on reception and they never left the bag individually, always sticking together with some God knows what. These pictures were either sent in by the wives or more usually the sad naked man himself, standing in front of a mirror. Their faces were either fully on show, usually a proud Mr Big Dick, obscured by the reflection of the cameras flash or scratched into obliteration.

Another new boy job was picking the wife pictures that were sent in their thousands, enough to fill the 'Readers Wives' section and a couple of Readers Wives Special magazines every year. Again in their little individual bags and again in a dirty great cardboard box you didn't want to put your hand in.

One of the ladies I recognised, the address written on the back was on the estate where I lived, about five roads away. She was a nurse on my Mum's ward when she had her hysterectomy, what a small world.

Another noticeable one was 'Rose from Gloucester,' in the background of her pictures you could see her house was a mess, it looked like a building site! She went on to be very famous, on everyone's lips. The police came and took her pictures away.

A contender for the weird prize, was an oriental lady that sent a picture of herself squatting over a toilet with her feet on the seat, legs akimbo and an impressively large un-pinched poo hanging between her legs. There was no address, but on the back she'd written in Biro,
'I lik tis one, you tink I look like monkey wid tail?'
We weren't allowed to use that one and it's something I've never been able to unsee.

In my humble opinion the girls in the magazines weren't exploited, there was no way we were stereotyping or projecting a perfect image of the female form, quite the opposite, these magazines celebrated the female form in all its shapes, colours and sizes, and encouraged them all to show the world what real women looked like.

These were the days way before the internet came and provided the really good stuff. The days when a fanny had hair, no one had an arse-hole and nipples were banned from the cover. Even a girl just pulling her knickers too hard, creating labial separation, would be rejected by the distributer, this was called 'Taking in Washing'.

Shaven Havens was another very popular special edition we published. The photographers would come in with a case of transparencies from all the shoots they'd done and we'd have a look on the light box. The first set they showed us was always their best, a very heavily pubed young lady playing with a can of shaving foam. She'd start by lathering up, a bit of writhing about with puppy eyes to the camera, then a shave, resulting in a nice smooth fanny like a split tennis ball, clean as a whistle.

This was fine until you got to the next few shoots, there was different underwear, different settings and the same model, but never a big bushy before shot. All they did was cover the already shaven fanny in foam and scrape the foam off again and again, our readers weren't stupid they would never fall for that.

Another favourite were the messy specials, our number one model used to phone the editor up with her own suggestions of what she wanted to be covered in. She was Doris, a septuagenarian legend, with thinning old lady hair and a very Rubenesque figure, like a big cuddly nanny. She'd request things like baked beans, we'd get loads of catering tins, a free-standing bath and she would tip them all over herself. Sometimes she'd

even bring her middle-aged daughter in to join her shoot. She
never wanted money, she did it all for a bottle of Jack Daniels
and a lift to the station.

At the porn palace we had recently started a magazine for
women. It still had to be sold on the top shelf but it was
marketed as the stylish option for ladies, to see artistically lit
naked men, not just another gay mag.

The editor was a rough as ya like Scot, she pulled no punches,
took no prisoners and had a filthy mouth you wouldn't kiss your
mother with. Her assistant on the other hand was a wannabe
IT girl, a brain of mashed potato and the personality of a piece
of toilet paper. She name dropped loads of now dead coke
heads from her circle of friends, mostly from the society pages,
impressing no one.

One of their first shoots in our studio was with a bloke called
Kerry, a martial artist and a proud contestant on Gladiators.
The editor was hoping that her readers would love him as much
as he loved himself. His bravado seemed to dip a little when he
found that his path to fame, fortune and females, involved him
being oiled up and wrapped head to toe in cling-film.
It was hilarious when we saw the pictures, a cock and balls
doesn't look great at the best of times but they reach a whole
new low within an oily wrap, his pride and joy looked like an
off-cut offal selection in a council estate butcher's window.

We got wind that we were going to be subject of a Channel 4
documentary, partly we thought because we now presented
the new perspective that a woman's porn mag provided.
The enthusiasm from management was met with complete
indifference from the staff, no-one wanted to be seen
advertising the fact they worked in porn. Sue, one of the
designers, said they could film over her shoulder as she laid out

a spread on the drawing board as long as her face wasn't shown.

On the day of filming we were told to tidy up and get rid of any hardcore pictures on the wall, of which there were many. Above my desk I had a couple of pictures from some German magazine, one of them we had titled 'Pen Tidy.' Basically it was the close-up of a woman's chuff stuffed with 30 to 40 felt tip pens, very colourful and quite abstract, but if you really looked you could make out what it was, when you spotted the stretched podge, pubes and arse-hole at the bottom of the pic.

The other pic wasn't abstract at all, a close up of a woman's head surrounded by six spunking cocks, she had a lovely big smile and a face like a plasterer's radio. I thought I'd leave these pictures up until someone noticed, they never did. It felt like a little two fingers to the censors but I wasn't sure the camera even saw them.

When the programme was aired there they both were, right above Sue at the drawing board, I can't believe no-one noticed. I had managed to get Hardcore German porn, completely uncensored on Channel 4.

In all the years I worked at the porn palace, we only ever had one Christmas party, a lavish do at the local Chinese, a very expensive and highly rated restaurant.

This was one of the occasions when we got to experience the legendary alcohol capacity of the Editor in Chief, he was only mid 30s but his doctor said he had the body of a man more than twice his age. The years he spent working in Fleet Street, with their pub culture probably didn't help.

He lived in a lovely market town in Suffolk, but only had a branch line between work and home, each having a pub next to the station. One time he missed the last train and bummed an early hours lift home with a bloke who had a Porsche. He left his briefcase in the car, he'd never met the bloke before so hadn't a clue where his case was.

Another time he and his wife woke up pissed on Saturday afternoon. They'd drunk so much that they couldn't remember who they'd left the kids with, they had to phone round all their friends to see where they were.

The best story though was when he needed a piss in the middle of the night, he opened his bedroom window and pissed on the pavement below, he fell out the window and broke his neck, laying there with his PJs around his ankles on the main road into town in a puddle of his own piss. He survived and is OK now, but has limited movement in his neck.

We'd already had too much to drink trying to keep up with Ed, when Timbola pointed out to me that the ornate wooden screens that we were sat next to, not only shielded the dining area from the toilets, but also shielded the diners from the restaurant's collection of wine bottles. They were clearly visible underneath. We took it in turns to pick imaginary things up from the floor and liberated quite a few of the bottles over to our side. When you're pissed you think you're invisible, we clearly weren't and realised that when we noticed two of the waiters just standing there watching us. The one on the left gave us a sneaky thumbs up then pointed to his pad, informing us it was all being added to the bill.

In the end everyone of our table of 12 had a bottle or two to take home and the bosses bill was nearly a grand more than he thought it'd be.

That night me and Timbola started one of our traditions that carried on for a number of years. I went to the toilet and he was standing drunkenly at the door peeling the metal Gents signs off, he lifted his shirt and said,

'Quick stick it on my back!'
We forgot all about it till the next day, when he called me and
said his wife had cut her hand on it, finding it still stuck to his
back the next morning.

In the back of all our adult titles, there were pages and pages
of sex toys and marital aids. There were Dildos, Dildon'ts, Butt
Plugs, Whips, Straps, Lubes and Tubes. Basically anything you
ever wanted to stick up yourself or stick up her, put your cock
in or put around your cock. From Nipple Tassels to Blow-Up
Dolls we advertised them all.

One of the funniest was a female torso, it was just the crotch
area, as if you'd sliced a woman in half at the belly button then
chopped the legs off, leaving just the waist and toilet parts. The
unique selling point to this object, was that it had...
'A Realistic Vagina with Real-Feel Pubic Hair!'
I knew my Mum and Dad were coming over that evening, so to
try and shock Mum, I'd take a magazine home and show her the
sex toys available.

A very intelligent lady is my mum, she's very artistic and
scientific. She worked in the labs at the hospital, so was very
hard to shock. She could talk at length on any number of
subjects and often did. It has been said,
'Ask her the time and she'll tell you how to make a watch!'

That evening, I'd furnished them both with a cup of tea and
showed Mum the magazine. I drew her attention to the Blow up
Dolls, especially the Real Feel Pubic Haired torso. I waited for
any little signs of shock but she completely turned the tables on
me! 'Oh that's bad,' she said, 'It's like one we had at work.'
I had to ask, 'What?'
'There was a poor woman in the hospital, who had a massive
cancerous tumour removed, we had it in the Lab. It was exactly

like that, they had to remove a lot of stomach tissue right down to the leg, you could see the vagina too. The only difference is our one was in a bucket!'

I knew I stood little chance of shocking her, but I didn't expect to be owned so badly by my Mum.

My brother had tried it a few years back, when he found out that she did sperm counts. He kept asking her to do a sperm test on his man milk. At first she said it wasn't allowed. After he kept asking, she just told him,

'If I tested your sperm, all you want me to say is,

'Wow your sperm is great! You've got the best swimming sperm I've ever seen!' If you didn't have any sperm, I wouldn't tell you anyway, so forget it!'

Mum later admitted that she could have done a sperm test for him. One of the other lab technicians was trying to get pregnant and she brought in a sample from her husband in a yoghurt pot. I was wondering if the husband knew or had she milked him into the yoghurt pot one night when he was asleep?

In my early twenties, sometimes months of celibacy passed without even the sniff of a fragrant female wafting their heady scent into my life. Having my own car and one bedroom starter home, I thought it shouldn't be such a struggle.

I din't think I was too ugly on the eye, sure puberty hit me pretty hard and I was blessed with more than my fair share of body hair, but that shouldn't put them off until I'm standing naked in front of them.

My penis is a good enough handful I think, not the biggest in the world but you wouldn't want it up your nose as a wart. My dad always told me that more than three inches hurts a girl and I wasn't wanting to hurt anyone. It must be either my personality or maybe women can mind read and sense all the different things I wanted to do to them. I eventually realised that if I didn't meet my perfect match at work or between home and the beer in Tesco then we'd never meet.

A work liaison was out of the question due to the lack of anyone being remotely attractive. Also I was always told never to shit on your own doorstep. That was until the publishers where I worked received a job application for an Editorial Assistant on one of their Hair Magazines.

A young girl, only 21 from Braintree. The best thing about her was her name, Evelyn Bumgardner! No one believed the Editor in Chief when he told us but we all passed her CV around and felt like we knew her before she'd even stepped inside the building. The Editor in Chief's office was the venue for the interview, it was off a corridor with windows that ran along its length. During the interview three or four of us took it turns to go past the windows to have a butchers at Evelyn and try and put Ed off.

We all knew that Braintree girls had a reputation for being rough, a well renowned hotbed for inbreeding. Usually by the age of 21 a Braintree girl would have three kids from three different fathers, and three pairs of chocolaty hand-prints all over the arse of her grubby leggings. Hair scraped back so tight it caused a permanent smile and enormous Elizabeth Duke hooped earrings adorning a gum chewing jawline.

This girl was different though, when we were expecting mutton we were presented with lamb. Where we expected a bit of old Scrag End we got a succulent Rump.

Her succulent Rump was just the start, it led the eye down a slender leg on to an expensively shod foot. Her face was beautiful, shiny dark brown hair cascading onto the collar of a dog tooth, woollen matador style jacket. The hair framing a film star face with a ski jump, be-freckled nose and maybe just a few too many teeth in her mouth. Her deep brown, heavily lashed giraffe eyes, complementing a face I wanted to wake next to.

The result of her Zeppelin racing breasts was a draw and completed the most stunning hourglass figure I think I'd ever seen, the sand equally distributed and defying gravity. She had the poise and elegance of Audrey Hepburn in Breakfast at Tiffany's and I was hooked. If only I could get a woman so perfect, if only she'd Breakfast at Wendell's then my life would be complete!

After the interview we pressed the Ed,
'Well? Has she got the job?' We asked as one.
He said yes, he thinks so, great we thought. Then he dropped the bombshell that rocked my world,
'She's a vegetarian!' My heart sank.

That evening I had a long hard think over a can of own-brand lager, this was the girl that I'd been waiting for all my life, so what if she's was a veggie? At least she's not a vegan and someone mentioned that she did eat fish. I made it my life's goal to snare this prize specimen.

Using my full arsenal of bullshit, humour and sincerity, I gradually wore her down and within a year my house was adorned with all the cushions, candles and wallpaper borders I never knew it needed, she'd moved in! Her standards were obviously a lot lower than I first thought.

It had taken me 24 years to find Miss Right. Little did I know that her first name would be Always!

8 Snooker

Me and Timbola quite often escaped the better halves with a few hours at the tables in the snooker club. One club we frequented was the same as my Father Midget-in-Laws. It was a nice, no frills club, we knew the owner and most of the other patrons, it was just like a giant man cave.

Every Wednesday Father Midget-in-Law and his two mates played in the local league, he kept on about me and Timbola starting a team and joining. The format was that each team had three players, each playing three frames, the tables were free but the home team had to provide food for the opposing team. Our club only charged a fiver for a plate of rolls for everyone.

We liked the idea and knew a few mates that played snooker, we just didn't want to be with them every week. Father Midget-in-Law said he knew someone who'd stepped in for him a few times when he needed a reserve player. We reluctantly agreed to meet him. Expecting another coffin dodger friend of his who'd spend more of the evening trying to get some wee out than playing snooker.

Surprisingly we both took to Bob straight away, he was only

our age, a massive 6'5" man mountain, he had a mother nature forced shaved head and a sense of humour that fitted ours, a very rare occurrence for me and Timbola. He bought the first round, seemed to know all the locals and we chatted like old friends.

We found out by the end of the evening, that he owned a main car dealership locally that I knew, and funnily enough my Dad had told me stories about it when we drove past it as kids. When my dad was a little he used to spend holidays staying with his Auntie Ethel. The man next door had one of the biggest cars at the time, a Mark X Jaguar, my dad loved it. That man used to own Big Bob's garage in the 1960s, I told him and Bob said it was his dad's car, he used to live next to Auntie Ethel when he was small.

The big man was an impressive snookerist, his only drawback being his temper, if Timbola or I missed a sitter we'd tell each other they're shit and playing like a spastic. Bob on the other hand would slam the cue down and get so angry with himself, we'd never had a sense of being that bothered, to us snooker was just an excuse to be out of the house. We all agreed to try the league and told the club owner he had a new E team next year if he wanted one.

My Dad was taking early retirement and was offered the option to buy his company car at a very good price. I wanted to have it, being only three years old, fully serviced and only Dad had ever driven it, but I could only afford the car if it was on finance. I didn't have the cash that his company wanted. Bob said he'd buy the car and provide finance, the first of many car situations he solved over the next few years.

One thing I had always been wary of was second hand car dealers, now I had someone I could trust and he was a main dealer. It took all the stress away, sure I ended up buying more cars than I ever intended but I never had to leave his forecourt in a tiny courtesy car with stickers all over it. I'd always get either Bob's or his wife's personal drive.

Over the years I had a Range Rover, big Mercedes, Audi Quattro, numerous Jags, including a 5lt XJS convertible. On the downside there was one time I was driving back from Ikea one Saturday and I was bursting. I only stopped at Bob's to have a piss and say hello but I left having bought his wife's E Class Mercedes. It's amazing what you can afford when your mate's doing your credit application.

After I'd bought a couple of cars from him it all got very routine, I'd go in to pick up a new car, we'd chat and pass the time, then he'd just hand me my new keys. I used to ask if I needed to sign any paperwork, he'd just say no you've already signed everything and been accepted for finance, I'd just drive it away.

Over the years the three of us had some good times, our team moved up the snooker league, somehow managing to gain premier league status. Never being in the position to challenge for anything but we always achieved an impressive lower to mid table mediocrity.

Many a drunken evening was spent round each others houses and even the wives seemed to tolerate each other. Bob's house was the best to visit, a big house with a big garden and a big drum kit.

The Timbola household was funny, all their children were boys and all as fertile as Timbola, The front room had three bunk beds to accommodate all offspring and grand offspring. Not being a massive dog lover I was always wary of Arnie their Staffordshire Bull Terrier, but he was usually put in his place under the stairs.

Apart from one night, in the early hours we were around the dining table playing cards when I felt a heavy warmth on my lap, looking down hoping to see my drunken wife's foot playing keepy uppy, I lifted the tablecloth and there was Arnie. His head was wider than it was high, his dribbly mouth full of bollock tearing teeth smiling up at me.

I felt strangely safe having his jaw on top of my cock and balls, but I knew Staffs were quick and genetically programmed not to let go, if he did ever get the taste for my succulent undercarriage. I think my hanging beef went sumo style on me that night as I spent most of the next morning coaxing my testicles down back into their little hairy hammock.

9 Chimney

My last car purchase from Big Bob's garage was driving perfectly, until I realised the speed shown on my TomTom wasn't the same as the cars speedo. I'd spent the last couple of month driving 10mph faster than I'd thought.

He took the car in and we were waiting for the part, I didn't mind, I had his Jag courtesy car, no hardship on my part. Then I got a call from him, a serious voice that he'd never used before, he said he'd had to shut up shop, lay everyone off and that I should come and get my car before the receivers took everything over.

The new part was in the boot and the Colchester main dealer knew the situation and was expecting a call from me. A bit shocked, I went straight round to get a synopsis of the situation from him, but he wasn't really wanting to talk. I offered my 'If there's anything I can do, call me,' textbook niceties and drove off in my car, leaving a clearly broken man.

I heard nothing for quite a few weeks, until I chanced upon his wife near the onions in Sainsbury's, just between the leeks and parsnips. Obviously I asked after him and said should I call?

She said a very definite No! and that he's not taking it well, he's got really bad depression. This was years before depression got as mentioned as it is today, I wouldn't have known what to say anyway.

It was a year before the big man came back to us. He seemed OK, his family now living in his Mums old house, the business gone and franchise gone. He managed to keep some commercial property that he rented out. His wife had been bookkeeping locally since the garage shut, he'd passed some electrical qualification and was trying his hand at fitting kitchens and bathrooms, he always was very handy.

He wanted some printing to advertise his new venture, so of course I obliged. I could tell he was putting on a brave face, he had lost the old swagger. It didn't seem right when he drove off in his white Escort van, not a Range Rover like the good old days, but good luck to him, at least he'd turned the corner and was back in contact with the world.

Our meetings became less and less frequent over the next couple of years. Then out of the blue, I'd just finished my first day back at work after the Christmas break and I came home to a hand delivered letter on the matt, no stamp. It was from Bob's wife.

It started with apologies for this letter being so late, then… 'I'm sorry to say we lost Bob before Christmas.' Dead? I read on. in a nut shell it said - He's going up the chimney tomorrow, can I tell Timbola and the Midget in-Laws. A bit of a bombshell to put it lightly, I made the calls, spending most of the evening on the phone.

Mr and Mrs Timbola picked me up from work the next day as it was on their way to the crematorium. We knew most of the faces, obviously my in-laws, his sister, all the boys from the garage and snooker club, but the hardest to acknowledge were

his three children. The eldest was just 16, about to face a year of
exams, having to look after her little brothers and wave their dad
goodbye. There wasn't a dry eye in the house as she stood in
front of a sea of mourning heads, choking back the tears.
She did her reading, I don't know how, I couldn't do that.

Anyway, the Wi-Fi in the crematorium was a fucking joke so we
all had to sit and listen to the penguin do the God bits. Timbola
nudged me and pointed to a line at the bottom of the Order of
Service handout, 'All donations to be made to MIND.'
It was only then that we both realised he'd topped himself!

After the service we all did the funeral shuffle past the oven
curtains to the outside, we really wanted to know what had
happened, but now didn't seem the time to ask. We knew no
details at all, one day we're told he's dead, the next day he's a
cloud of dust floating on the wind. We did the sad smile, widow
hug and everyone gradually scattered back to their cars and got
on with life.

We remained in a state of ignorance until two or three months
later when the Midget-in-Laws produced a cutting from the
local newspaper.
'Woman steals over £240,000 from employer!' Adorning the
story was a great big mug shot of Bob's wife looking like a
inmate from Prisoner Cell-block H.

Evidently, she'd been working as the bookkeeper at a chicken
sexing agency, and over the last five years had been helping
herself to a quarter of a million quid! 'To fund her lavish
lifestyle' it said. Bob had been a Personnel Manager there, his
charges had been dropped when he took his own life. He was
found apparently, with a hosepipe going from the exhaust into
the car, it said.

Bob was one person that we thought would be safe picking up
soap in a prison shower, but obviously the thought was too

much for him. His wife ended up with 3 years inside then out on license.

The year after we had to say goodbye to a less suspicious friend of ours, Mels Bells. She was a lovely bubbly personality and the wife's best friend since school.

She had travelled the world after university finally settling in Boston, US of A, living with an American family as their nanny. At first we'd maybe see her once a year when she was home visiting her parents. She'd stay at ours for a couple of days and my job was to keep their wine flowing, as they were busy drink-smoke-dancing to Abba in the garden.

She eventually moved to London and got a good job in the City, living first in Crouch End in a shared house, then her own flat half way up the Harringay Ladder.

We'd moved to a quaint little market village in Essex often seen in Lovejoy. It had numerous antique shops, three Pubs, a Chippy, a Chinese, an Indian and a famous Restaurant that Michael Caine used to own, all within three minutes stumble from our house.

When Mel walked home to her flat from the tube in London, she'd pass junkies shooting up, any little handkerchief of grass was littered with used needled and empty tins of Wife-beater. In contrast, we'd walk round the corner to pick up our curry and there'd be a couple of teens knocking back a fruity yoghurt drink, then they'd put the empty pots in the bin.

After only a few visits Mel wanted a piece of the action, and it was not too long before we were helping her move into a little 500 year old beamed cottage, just around the corner from us.

A large amount of time was spent in The Chapel, a great socialising pub that embraced the old English tradition of

Ye Olde Lock-in. Many a morning the three of us we're rolling ourselves home at three or four in the morning along any available fence or wall.

Sunday was Quiz Night and we did really well for a team of just three, our main rivals were another team of three locals, who just had the edge over us in number of wins. After the quiz finished, any rivalry went and we finished off the night with them. It was one of them that Mel ended up marrying, after a lot of not so subtle pushing together from the wife.

After a while we moved out of the village, but the girls still had their salad and wine evenings together. On one of them I'd been asked if I minded driving Mel, she'd hit the kerb a couple of times recently and was worried about her eyesight. She wasn't the most confident driver at the best of times.

We thought she just wanted a drinky night and didn't want to drive, but it ended up being a very aggressive brain tumour. In no time she was gone too. Another trip to the crematorium, for us to wave off another one gone far too soon. There are loads of people I'd rather wave off up the flue, but it always seems to be the good ones.

The wake was at Mel's house, all her gym buddies and girls from work were there, leaving me only her husband and family that I knew to chat to.

I went to the car for a can of coke and a breather from the solemn atmosphere, only for it to explode when I opened it. I quickly put it back in the cup holder still fizzing over, hand on top to try and quell the eruption. Checking the door pockets and glove box for tissues to mop up the mess, all I could find was the wife's emergency supply of two tampons, under the service manual next to the locking wheel nut and half a packet of Starburst.

I unwrapped one and dried my hands with it, expecting a bit of comedic swelling but nothing really. Lifting the can out, I dried its outside then dropped the mousey into the coke puddle, I looked in wonder as the little brown pool engorged the tampon, its volume tripled and the puddle was no more.

To say I was impressed with the Lilets Super Plus tampon is an understatement. If I was a girl, it would certainly be my tampon of choice for my monthly mess and it well deserves its four drops out of five rating on the side of the packet.

I lifted the tampon up and the coke had completely gone, to my amazement not a drip from my sanitary product, I locked the car and went to put it in the kitchen bin.

Just my luck that four girls had stopped for a chat next to the wine supply. I was small talking for a good ten minutes with whoever they were, trying to shield my soggy friend behind my back, waiting for them to fuck off and mingle but they didn't. Then another joined the wine club from behind and asked why I was holding a used brown tampon behind my back.

I didn't think I could ride this one out so I just said,
'Oh yeah, I was looking for the bin.'
From then on I was referred to as Mr Tampon, embarrassing, but at least it lightened the mood a little.

10 Cambridge

After a few years at the publishers the gang started leaving, no one senior was being replaced, so there were no prospects of promotion for the remainers. We hadn't had a pay rise for three years and the moral was at an all time low.

I was getting itchy feet and Timbola, who'd already left, had tales of how much he was earning freelancing in London, I had to try it before I took root. A few recommendations from him to his agencies, opened the doors for me and I ended up on the books of three good agencies in the smoke.

There seemed to be a load of freelancers really taking the piss, trying to pass themselves off as designers, but in reality knowing fuck all. When the clients were faced with someone who turned up on time, could do the job and could actually design, they loved you and gave you repeat bookings, requesting you by name month after month.

I turned down quite a few permanent job offers from the clients, I was liking the random nature of the freelance world too much and the money was more than double I was used to, even after travelling expenses were taken into account.

My best three weeks was a 9am to 5pm stint in Old Street,
retouching photos for Design Week, after a full days work
I'd then get on a tube to Edgware Road, where from 6pm till
3am in the morning I would do another days work, cutting out
the background of toy photographs for the Argos catalogue,
earning double time. Timbola was just working the night shift
and gave me a lift home to Colchester at 3am, I'd sleep in the
car on the way back, then grab another couple more hours
at home.

Then up for the train at 7.30am to London, to do it all again
the next day. I managed this for three weeks and by the end I
couldn't tell you my name I was so tired, but it did pay for a
week in a private villa in the hills above Cannes. Me and the
wife rattling about in 4 bedroom luxury villa with our own
private pool.

One of my other regular monthly jobs was a week at Camden
Council, designing The Camden Citizen, their council
newspaper. I had my regular desk amongst the Media Team next
to a larger than life, in every way, black girl called Blossom.
She was hilarious, very loud and evidently best friends with
Ian Wright the Gooner.

The only other white faces in Media were a really nice young
dad that supported Watford and Bruce who dealt with filming
permits in area. He signed off the Spice Girls first video in
St Pancreas Station, that was opposite the council offices.
Often the three of us would chat about how hard it was
being the ethnic minority at work, we were always going to be
different and stand out in the Council offices, being white,
able bodied and being able to speak English.

Everyone was nice to us, both the walking and wheelchair
disabled, all the nationalities and even those that couldn't speak
English, they were all very welcoming.

An exciting Monday started when I had to fight through a hoard of reporters and camera crews to get to the main lobby of the council offices. I got my pass from security and entered the lift, there I found out that a syndicate of 15 from one of the housing departments had won over £25 million in the lottery. When I got to the media offices they were swamped, the phone never stopped ringing and evidently not one of the winners had plans to quit their job, what dedication to the cause.

I saw just enough of London in the two years I freelanced, basically the journey to the client and the journey back to Liverpool Street, that was enough for me. When you have to walk past prostitutes having a piss in the streets behind Kings Cross and the great unwashed asking for cash all the time, London soon loses its magic.

Couple this with waiting for a train with standing room only that might not come, and the three hours of your life spent travelling that you'll never get back, the city was losing its appeal and it was Timbola that came to my aid again.

An old editor friend from the porn palace, was now working just outside Cambridge, for a company that did the telephone sex chat lines that you see in the back of glossy magazines and papers. He asked Timbola if he was still freelancing as he needed a freelance designer for a couple of months.

Timbola was happy with his daily routine and didn't want to change. I on the other hand fancied a change and would rather spend an hour a day driving to work in my car, than standing with the brain dead souls, under the armpit of someone who clearly hadn't showered, on a train. He passed him on to me and I gratefully accepted the gig.

The company sprawled itself over five or six units in a modern courtyard setting, all units were interlocking, a confusing rabbit warren of offices, meeting rooms and kitchens. The boss in his

boardroom sat over the arch you had to drive through to get
parked. There was a recording studio with sound booth for the
recorded chats, offices on the second floor then on the third,
the boys and girls that did the live chats in the eaves under
the roof. Going in there was like walking into the alien cafe in
Star Wars. They all had lovely voices I'm sure, but if you could
see them while having a sexy chat, now that would be a very
challenging wank!

The big boss had started the company with a few strippers that
he toted around the East End in the early 80s. When their show
had finished and the girls where having a drink at the bar, all
the punters would swarm over them, buying them drinks and
drunkenly try and get their phone numbers. The Boss had cards
printed for them to give out, with telepone numbers on. The
drunks getting a card and thinking they're on a promise, left
them alone. If they did try to call the numbers on the cards they
were put through to a premium rate line, costing them a fortune.
He soon stopped pimping strippers around town, sat them at a
phone and waited for the money to roll in. He was now driving
a big white Bentley and he, his wife and their girlfriend all lived
and worked together.

My job was to help someone called Brin, designing the
telephone chat ads, a funny bloke in his mid 30s with a natural
talent for being the victim of a practical joke. He'd laugh with
you at himself, not knowing what was being laughed about. He
was innocent like a five year old, but had the mind of a 60 year
old hippy. He still lived with his Mum and believed that all his
siblings, with their wives and kids, should live in a commune
with their Mum. Everyone giving their wages to the Mother
every month, who'd then decide what it was spent on.

Tim didn't have a design background and really appreciated
any little tips I gave him. His previous job was working for the

Ordinance Survey map people. He went very quiet when we were talking about the war in Kuwait and Iraq, we were amazed at the accuracy of these missiles we watched on the news.

He said it was even more amazing that they hit anything, because the missiles were programmed with data from the Ordinance Survey were he used to work. They had digitised that whole area and he admitted that most of the time, if it was desert he wouldn't bother doing it at all, thinking no one would ever go there to check any missing sand dunes or little tiny roads.

I worked a month and a half in Cambridge then had to return back to London, really missing being able to drive to work.

Then, out of the blue the Cambridge mob contacted me, saying they had a new venture that involved 'The Internet.' It sounded very interesting but I knew nothing about it, I'd heard of it and was interested and told them as much. My contact was the bosses girlfriend, a cute little Irish girl, very pleasing on the eye but also a very scary business orientated professional.

They had a client who owned most of Soho, he wanted to put online versions of their magazines on the internet. She assured me that she knew nothing either and that we'd learn together. There would be our fist experience of a tekkie joining us, who knew how to build a website and together the three of us would take on this World Wide Web.

I accepted the job, everyone was saying that the internet was the future, if you could put pictures and magazines on a website and take money from people in the privacy of their own home, what else could you do? It was mind-boggling! Someone even said that soon you'd be able to do your shopping on the computer, and have it delivered to your house. Yeah right, as if!

Our Tekkie Russell was at first helpful, we were not now

designing for A4 pieces of paper in millimetres, but for a 640x480 screen resolution that's in pixels, different from what we knew but we sort of got it.

Then we were told everything we wanted to do would take too long to download, as people only had 56k modems. Any animations or videos would take ages to download and show on screen. How could you get people to pay for this? We were between us, starting to have our doubts about the future of this stupid internet thing.

Things progressed and we started to get the hang of it, as the work increased and our client was getting more and more online subscriptions we employed more Designers and more Tekkies. As we got to know more of these strange 'Tekkie' creatures, the more we realised that their second priority was to be helpful and do the work, their first was to keep what they did and how they did it a secret, if they didn't let on how simply things could be done, they thought they'd be indispensable.

We grew as a company quickly and I had to start advertising for Designers, and of course interviewing. Opening all the letters for applications was a laborious task, so in the advert I started asking for relevant experience, a CV and their three favourite jokes, just to relieve the boredom.

The amount of racist, disgusting and sick jokes people sent, really was amazing. I pissed myself laughing at quite a few, obviously not the racist ones, but who was stupid enough to put offensive jokes in a job application? We had all the words in there, the N word and the P word, Fuck, Shit, Wank, Tit, Cunt, Bum, Arsehole, and even worse Paddy. This was not a good idea when the boss is Irish and very quickly edited the list of maybes.

There was one application that did stand out, a six page hand written letter with doodles sent by a girl in the village. Her one joke was, 'Do you like camping? I ask tentatively.'

There was a picture of me, labelled 'Wendell', running from a spider, underneath she had written, 'I didn't know you were afraid of spiders!' Finally there was a picture of a princess kissing a frog under her sign off.

She said she knew all the programs asked for and that she'd work for nothing. I showed the boss as a joke, but she latched onto the 'Work for Nothing' sentence.
'We should get her in, just see what she's like!'
I said that if she's interviewed you're doing it alone, I wanted no part of it.

The girl arrived and within five minutes the boss called me, saying, 'You got to come and help, she's a fucking nutter. I don't know what to do!'
I went to the meeting room and was introduced as being in charge of the studio. The girl looked like a Glastonbury reject, big flowery dress, denim jacket and her sandals on the floor, next to where she was sitting barefoot. I asked to see her portfolio and she said,
'It's this.' Handing me a rolled up piece of A4 paper.
It was a bad pencil drawing of a dog, above it the word LOST and below her telephone number.

Trying not to laugh I asked,
'Did this work? Did you find the dog? She said no.
When I asked if she worked on an Apple Mac she looked confused and said I think so.

To piss off the boss, I suggested we go to the studio and see what she could do. I sat her down in front of my computer she looked like a stoned puppy, she couldn't even wake it up, she moved the mouse about a bit, which was promising, but said, 'It's not the same as mums, but I pick things up really quickly.' We thanked her and said we'd be in touch.

One guy that grabbed our attention was Captain from Manchester, he applied for an Account Handler/Editor position, his whole personality was forged in The Hacienda and he was definitely having it large. He was a caricature Manc, could have been from Oasis. He turned up to the interview obviously hung over, he had a plaster above his left eye because his mates had shaved one eyebrow the night before, when they found out he had an interview.

He was hired more for the fact he was a laugh and it would be a crack having him around, than his CV or qualifications. After a few nights out with him we realised that he supplemented his income with a bit of Class A toilet economics, he was a bit of a live-wire himself, no one was surprised.

He seemed to know everyone who worked the doors of every club in town, we never had to queue, just strolled straight in with Captain like VIPs. You could bet though that within five minutes, someone would be shouting that they're gonna kill him and he'd be off down the street.

On the odd occasion when he hadn't been threatened with death and stayed with us the whole night, he really come to the fore. After the clubs had kicked out and the kebabs were flowing, walking past flailing arms of non-contact fighting drunks and girls pissing between cars, he still promised somewhere we could get a drink.

We went into a tiny chip shop housing a couple of drunks trying to eat chips, but really just painting their faces in ketchup. He had one of his words in a China man's ear and a door was opened for us to go through. Down a corridor past bags of potatoes, through two more doors and we were at the top of a massive iron staircase, overlooking a vast warehouse. The whole floor area filled with row after row of trestle tables and at least 200 Chinese faces all drinking, smoking and gambling, a nice place to round off the morning we thought.

True to his Manc roots, Captain always prided himself on being able to lay his hands on hooky stuff, or 'Merchandise' he preferred to call it, Perfume, Designer Clothes with dubiously stitched labels and Jewellery. One morning he entered the room and started his pitch,
'Hey lads, you know how much ya birds like Tiffany? Well look at this.' He reached into his sports bag and took out cream box after cream box, then some duck egg blue pouches all in the Tiffany style.
'Is this real or fake?' One of us asked. He looked hurt and said 'Lads, lads, lads, this isn't that fake shit! This is proper stolen from shops!'

Captain came to the aid of a lad at work, Bez, he was desperate for money as he owed his dealer/friend £500. His only real valuable possession was his souped up, boy racer, V6 VW Golf, fully loaded with a top of the shop stereo. The car obviously had a value but he couldn't sell it, no-one wanted a left hand drive rocket that had no history, and came from the continent, funny that. They hatched a plan, a bit of insurance fraud, what could go wrong?

Scouse Mickey, Captains mate, travelled down one night on the train, nicked Bez's car from outside his house, drove it back to Liverpool and torched it on the docks. The problem came when Bez tried to get his money, his insurance had lapsed a couple of weeks before and the car wasn't insured. This meant he now owed £500 to Scouse Mickey, £500 to his dealer and he didn't have a car or a nice stereo anymore. This sort of thing happened when Captain tried to help.

As the adult side of the company grew and ticked along nicely, a couple of Rain Man, skater boy Tekkies, had interested the boss with some encrypted something or other, that would enable the secure taking of credit cards over the internet. I was only involved in meetings because they needed a logo, literature and Corporate ID, it was very exciting stuff and the boss talked about how big this could get if we used his usual 'Throw everything at it' approach.

We bought one of the neighbouring units to distance the new respectable company from the old one, employed loads of serious middle-aged men in suits, all with a history in banking, some with personalities

We also employed a new breed of Tekkie, not the ones to build websites, this lot were from a completely different planet. When you are taking people's credit card numbers you needed serious, security savvy Tekkies. One of them stood out, he had a brain that worked in a way none of the others could even understand. We were told he was somewhere on the autistic register, he never made eye contact or talked to anyone and he looked like Jesus.

He had changed his name to that of a character from Star Trek and none of the others could use his keyboard, because he'd set it up using Klingon. Dressing completely in black, the only colour allowed anywhere near him was his nail varnish. He didn't just paint his very long fingernails, he pierced them too and had chains running here and there between his fingers. One of new, new-boys discovered that he had a personal website and after some searching we found it.

In real life he couldn't talk to people or look them in the eye, but my God, online he let it all hang out. There was a whole biography to his namesake from Star Trek, photos of him amongst other Goths at university, none of them interacting with each other or seeming to have fun, just sitting there being Goths.

There was a Q&A section on his website with quite a few questions being asked about the nail varnish he used, he had made a list:

1. Little finger left hand - Marzipan Meringue, L'Oreal.
2. Second finger left hand - Lemon Sorbet, No7.

All the way through to…

10. Little finger right hand - Enterprise Umber, Rimmel.

Then there was a list of each toe too!

He was asked about the way he dressed and revealed that anything made from Velvet, Silk or Nylon were his preferred garments, because he liked the way it felt against his skin. There was a whole page explaining why he liked fishnet stockings, a preference that we would never have guessed as he always wore big clumpy Doc Martens. The website was immediately everyones favourite and went straight into everyones bookmarks.

After a few months the skater boys dropped the bombshell that they were off to pastures new, that they couldn't give as much time to the project as it needed and they'd been offered £20,000 to do a Cornflake website. A very short sighted decision in the long run and we all thought the project was over.

To give them some credit, they recommended a Dutch man who knew the project and was keen to take over, a proper suited top Tekkie, a Lucid one that you could take to meetings with the banks. He soon took over the reigns and refreshingly made things a lot clearer to us non tekkies.

With all this added responsibility, the company had to take security very seriously, next to my office we had a secure server room, we couldn't get in we weren't allowed, it had bars on the window and key-coded door entry.

After one lunch I came back and the whole office smelled of Chinese food, we had a takeaway in the village and the policy was that, if anyone is getting Chinese for lunch, do the decent thing and ask if anyone wants anything. A battered ball or a noodle dish perhaps.

I stood at the door and said,
'Who's had Chinese?' No-one came the reply.
'C'mon now, I can smell Chinese someone's had one!'
Still no admission.
Jokingly I started going through peoples bins looking for evidence, nothing, now this is serious, I said.
'I can definitely smell Chinky who's had it? I wont be angry, just disappointed.'
All of a sudden a young Chinese girl came out of the server room, crying her eyes out, ran straight down stairs and out to her car. In the end no one had had a take-away and I'd upset the new girl on her first day.

The Christmas parties in Cambridge were legendary, the first couple of years they were held in the local village pub, we had a free bar, traditional turkey and all the trimmings and a chance to celebrate the birth of baby Jesus together.

As the company grew we had to use larger hotels in town that could accommodate the ever increasing number of employees. This was good because you could book a room and not have to worry about getting home, the rooms were discounted but we still had to pay. I did this for a couple of years when the hotels were three or four star, but as the company grew, money came rolling in and there was talk about floating on the stock market, the Hotel chosen was Cambridge's top five star.

The bosses had exiled themselves to Belgium in preparation of the floatation, when they came back they lived in five star luxury, the obvious place for them to hold the party.

This was too rich for me, I could justify £50 or £60 but this

was out of my league. One of the boys Jim, said he was putting
people up, so to save over £100 I booked myself a spot on his
floor with a few others.

The party was great, the misshapen girls from the top floor that
did the live telephone sex chat, were on form and embarrassing
themselves, even the boys who did the gay chat were being
unusually sociable.

Our moodiest two clients, Longdog and Kelly turned up with
their festive cheer, shaking everyone's hand as they mingled,
I shook Longdog's hand, 'Happy Christmas Wendell!' He said,
'Have a good one!' A strange handshake I thought, watching as
he went on to the next handshake, I opened my palm and there
was a little wrap of Class A something or other. As I watched
him shake numerous hands, half the recipients looked down
puzzled at their surprise gift, like me wondering what to do with
it, the other half just pocketed it like it was nothing special. I
gave mine to Waldo hoping it was cut with laxatives, he would
know where to stick it.

At the end of the party there was only me and Justin left,
putting the world to right and marking the girls out of ten.
We were both supposed to be staying at Jim's but they'd all left,
I remember them saying they were going, but forgot that I was
supposed to go with them.

Our new plan was that we get the train, it was only one stop to
Justin's house and the station was just round the corner from
the hotel we thought. It wasn't, it took ages, we were drunkenly
trudging through the slush on the pavement, it was snowing and
we only had shirts on, thinking we'd be in a taxi back to Jim's, it
was freezing.

The station was deserted, the last train went over an hour
before we got there and I'd had enough, I couldn't talk I was
so cold. Just said he thinks he could find our way back to Jim's

but wasn't sure. I was saying to leave me, I was happy to have a sleep on the platform bench, and wait till the morning, but Just, always Mr Positive said I'd die and that he'd get me there. For over an hour he kept saying,

'I'm sure it's up here,' or 'I recognise this bit', we were just wandering aimlessly, at one point he started knocking on random houses that had a light on.

'Hello, Happy Christmas, do you know where Jim lives please?' After numerous 'Fuck Offs!' We turned yet another corner and there was Jim's car, sitting outside Jim's house. We hugged and whooped like we'd struck gold.

We knocked on the door gently, we knew there were six people just the other side, someone would hear us. Nothing, we knocked louder, still nothing, I took the matter into my own hands, I said I was going to break the smaller bottom pane of glass, open the door and worry about it in the morning. It shattered with great volume into many pieces, we expected to be greeted with fury but at least we were out of the biting wind.

We crunched up to the final door between the hall and lounge, the little fuckers had locked that too, this was taking the piss! We thumped on the glass, shouting the names of those we knew were staying there, nothing. We couldn't stay on the floor of the hallway, that was covered in broken glass, I still had the rock in my hand and thought, bollocks, smashed the second pane of the night.

I turned the key through the door trying not to slash my wrists and we stepped into the lounge, three motionless sleeping bags on the floor, dead to the world. Sitting there on the sofa was Kev, smoking a joint! We stood there just staring at him for a good few seconds, as he took another toke.

'Why the Fuck didn't you open the door? How could you not hear us?'

'I thought you were burglars trying to break in! He squirmed.

I might have got an hour or so sleep that night and was woken by Jim screaming at Justin, out of the two of us he was the most likely to have smashed the windows. I calmed Jim down and said I'd call an emergency glazer and have it all good as new in no time. It was now Christmas Eve and the only glazer I could find, wanted £195 cash, to be fair to him within two hours it was all fixed.

The free food and drink at the party had cost me nearly £200 but at least I'd saved £120 by not staying at the hotel.

11 LJ

Once the wife had joined me as a thirty something, we re-assessed our oh-so-easy lives, both our biological clocks were ticking so loud it was keeping us up at night, so we decided to have a baby and she went and got herself pregnant.

One good thing about being a pregnant couple, is that opportunities arise to meet people you would otherwise never meet. We joined the NCT classes and met some very nice couples, we had a meeting every week and everyone was due to drop at roughly the same time.

In our group of six or seven couples, we had a very nice couple of Hippies, a Banker, an Architect, his wife was gorgeous, and the owner of a Mercedes dealership.

We did try the NHS class once at the hospital, where we met around 20 couples, a very nice couple on Methadone, a Wanker, an Archaeologist, his wife was hideous, and the owner of an arm full of needle marks.

We decided to just do the NCT classes, they were a bit more relaxed and you didn't have to pay for parking.

The other couples were all our age, early to mid thirties, we'd all reached the age when we could sit in a circle in a village hall and not be embarrassed to speak or ask questions.

We had various gatherings outside of the classes, one that we agreed to host, was the bra fitting party. The NCT lady organised a maternity bra specialist to come and measure the girls and their ever changing, shape shifting breasts. The men unfortunately had to go to the pub, where we got to know each other a bit better. I got chatting to the Architect and the Banker, my brother in law worked for a high street bank and had just been made redundant, I asked the banker if his job was safe or if he was worried about all the cuts being made. He said he hoped his job was safe, as he was one of the Directors of a Merchant bank in the city. These were the sort of people I should be mixing with.

One not so good thing about being a pregnant couple, is the people you are thrown together with when the little one decides he wants to come out. You're wife is put into a hospital bed next any old 'Random' that's about to drop, in our case the mother of twins.

The new mums, incarcerated next to each other for however long, are obviously going to chat, they're all going through the same thing so they can literally bounce off each other.
It's the fathers I feel for, we obviously have to visit at the same times, we just want to see the bubba and the wife, have a cuddle and ask about the washing machine, dishwasher and where things are in the house. What we don't really want, is having to converse with someone with no anecdotes, who wants a new best mate.

We saw the couple with the twins for a couple of years, just the odd weekend trip to the woods or a soft play area, when we had to. Before the twins had achieved 2 years, they'd added a daughter to their clan. They were always moaning on about how skint they were having two kids to feed, so we were surprised that they'd added another.

One day though they told us they'd come into some money from the government, quite a few grand.
'That could really help them out.' We thought, No, they went and bought a beach hut!

They said did we want to join them on Saturday and let the kids have a beach day, we accepted. The first thing we didn't realise was, they couldn't fit all three kids and child seats into their car, so we had to take the baby.

In their wisdom they had bought a people carrier but it only had one sliding rear door, it was on the drivers side. However many kids you had, they all had to be unloaded into traffic when you parked on the side of the road.

We drove off to the coast, the baby was no trouble and slept all they way next to our little LJ in his car seat. We got to Frinton and parked without a problem, there were enough spaces near us for them to park. After 10 minutes of standing around, we were wondering if we were in the right place, we definitely were, they definitely said Frinton. We tried calling their mobile but no answer. LJ and I were having a kick about on the grass with his little plastic football, when, after 50 minutes of waiting they turned up, he got out the car laughing.
'You'll never guess what I just did.' He said,
'I got onto the A12 and thought I was going to work, I'd gone all the way to Ipswich before I remembered we were going to the beach.' We all just looked at each other.

We had bag of toys, towels, buckets and spades and a windbreak, all he'd brought was a full size leather football, more for him than the twins. All their toys must be in the beach hut, we thought.

As we walked down the winding path to the sea, it was looking promising, the tide was out, the sun was out and there was a vast expanse of sand to play on.

We passed an old man walking his dog. Nodding hello politely, one of the twins suddenly grunted,
'Wooo, Waa, Wooo ,Wooo, Waa, Wooo!'
His brother went 'Nfurf Nfurf, Nfurf Nfurf!'
'Ha Ha,' he said, they always say 'Woof Woof' when they see a dog.
LJ and I just smiled, carrying on down the path, LJ tugged my hand and whispered,
'Daddy was that a Dalmatian? Like in the video?'
'Yes' I said, proud that our policy of talking to our son had actually been good for him and had stopped him from being a Mong!

The competitive dad went straight down to the beach shouting, 'Watch This!' To the boys.
He kicked his ball as far as he could, leaving his wife carrying the bag of sandwiches and the baby to the beach hut.

We were gasping for a coffee and were led to their beach hut, 'Ooh nice.' We said, making all the right noises, eager for a brew.
She rifled through her bag and shouted down to the beach, 'Have you got the keys?'
'No' came the reply, 'I thought you had them.'
'No I left them on the side for you.'
To cut a long, long days story short, they had no keys, this confirmed our thoughts about this couple and I don't think we ever saw them again. I just hope their kids grew up normal.
If they did it was despite their parents, not because of them.

12 Lakes

The In-laws were a funny stunted little couple, he was a retired wrestling toner salesman, he had five jokes that he had on a loop and repeated ad nauseam.

He was one of lifes performers and loved playing to a crowd. I think he meant well, but he could turn a whole room against him in five minutes with his racist ramblings, about how much better London used to be before 'they' move in, and why he hated disabled people in wheelchairs so much, that I took personal offense to.

She on the other hand, spent all her time apologising for him. Her whole married life was spent doing all the jobs he couldn't or wouldn't do. She was five foot nothing but could wire a plug, put up shelves, hang curtains, carpet a room and cook, he could just about boil an egg and if desperate butter a slice of toast.

Ever since they were first married, they'd gone to the Lake District on holiday every year with the kids, so my wife had loads of childhood memories of their camping trips. Now the kids had grown up and left home they went up more often, maybe three or four times a year, they'd shown me loads of photos but I couldn't see what all the fuss was about. There were nice hills and nice lakes then another couple of hills and another lake, I suppose it's the best that this country has to offer them, as he wouldn't fly.

LJ and I bought a nice big tent one year, he was now seven or eight, the perfect age for camping adventures. Even the wife was surprisingly positive about the thought of a week under Nylon, she needs make up doing every day and doesn't let go of her hair dryer for an hour in the morning, so I was quietly surprised.

It had been decided that we would go to the Lakes with the In-laws for a week. They knew a little village Inn they could stay at, we were booked into a camp site less than a mile away. Being mid 70s, they had their bladder requirements and we respected that.

Not having done the journey three times a year like them, they provided all the advice we could ever need about the where to stop services, where to fuel up services, where to eat services and don't take that road because we do this one. The journey was a couple of hours longer than I expected but the last half hour had some nice scenery with hills as we entered the fabled Lake District.

As we'd never organised a Lakes holiday the weeks itinerary was planned for us. We weren't visiting in the middle of summer, so nowhere had the infamous overcrowding that we'd have had if we'd gone in the height of the good weather.

We had a seven seat people carrier, so the in-laws kept their car at the Inn and came with us on days out. I was the driver with her dad next to me, giving me detailed directions. The Mrs was in the second row with her mum behind me, giving me detailed directions. Then LJ and Stanley Schnauzer in the third row at the back.

Over the week we really filled our days out, we went to the biggest lake in the Lake District, we went to the highest Lake in the Lake District, the deepest Lake in the Lake District, the longest Lake in the Lake District, a Lake that wasn't a Lake but a Water, the most photographed Lake in the Lake District and the Lake he wanted his ashes scattered into.

I think it was the day we went to the water speed record, Donald Campbell, Bluebird Lake that a grey cloud formed and the atmosphere changed. There were the usual 'holiday with parent' tensions bubbling under the surface. It was always going to happen, when you put two women together, neither of whom were ever wrong about anything, regardless that they were mother and daughter.
Us boys were keeping quiet, out the way, eggshell treading when her mum called the dog 'It!'
'IT!' She said 'IT has got a name, it's Stanley!'

It was a quiet drive to the next photo opportunity. On the way back to camp we detoured up a hill, stopping to have a coke and crisps in the highest pub in the Lake District. We came down the hill and were circumnavigating a pleasant little lake, the winding little road weaved itself alongside, just above water level, a tiny brick wall separating us.

Approaching a wooded area, still at lake level, the road widened a little but the cars had stopped. We were fourth or fifth in the queue and 100 meters ahead was a copper standing next to his flashing Police car, guarding a road closed sign.

A row of cottages stood, just back from the road on the right, overlooking the traffic jam and the lake behind. The people from the cottages were standing in their front gardens watching all the activity.

The in-laws were now both on edge, oldies never like an unexpected curve ball, a fly in the ointment of their plans.

Evidently we could either sit it out or go back the way we came,
that'd take 40 minutes, or another way, that'd be an hour.
It seems it couldn't have been a more awkward place to have
to stop.

I said that I'd ask the policemen about the situation and find out
how long the road would be closed, then we could decide what
course to take. I got out and walked round the back of the car,
making faces to LJ through the window as you do.

Just then a really funny looking jogger approached, running in
front of me as I got to the pavement.
She was a very big girl, sweating profusely and wearing a purple,
velvety sweatshirt and joggers, half of me was thinking,
'Good on her. She looks really funny but at least she's making an
effort.' The other half of me, was marvelling at her ridiculous
running action.

Her super-size legs were all over the place and the arms were
wind-milling like a bad Olympic swimmer.
I thought, 'I know, I'll make LJ laugh.'
I tapped on his window to get his attention, pointed to the
jogger, then I ran after the woman jogging, mirroring her
actions, I was about 10 paces behind.

My legs flailing side to side, my arms wind-milling like hers,
I looked at LJ over my shoulder and he was pissing himself
laughing. My job was done, I stopped my mimicking and
continued walking towards the policeman.

The jogger got to the policeman first, I saw him nod his head
slowly to the woman a couple of times, she just stopped and fell
to the floor, letting out a blood curdling scream!

I'd never heard anything like it before.
I stopped and as my brain pieced together the drama I was
experiencing in front of me. I realised that I had just taken

the piss out of a mother, whose kid had just been killed in the accident, causing the road to be closed.

It was a long, brisk walk of shame back to the car, my gaze never leaving the pavement. I was hoping the people in the queue hadn't put two and two together. Some people in the gardens were looking at me, some at the poor screaming woman I could still hear wailing behind me.

I reached the car expecting a bollocking from the wife, but they just asked what the policeman had said. They hadn't seen me, thank God, they were just discussing the plan of action.

I said it was a fatality and road would be closed a while, LJ shouted that was funny daddy from the back row, I smiled at him in the mirror and three point turned the hell away from there! The In-law sat-nav quickley recalculating the journey.

On the way back, the local radio said that the road was still closed, the fatality had been a 17 year old girl on a scooter, hit by car, she died at the scene.

13 Dad!

To make more use of the tent we found a couple of nice campsites just down the road in Suffolk. They were perfect for a long Bank Holiday weekend and we could be back home within an hour.

Once you'd come to terms with the camping way of life you settle in more quickly. You had to accept that people would stop and chat like old friends, especially when walking a Miniature Schnauzer. When you went to the toilet block with a loo roll under your arm, you accepted that everyone knew you were going for a shit.

I also found out, when you've put your 50p in the machine for a shower, outside the shower door, you're stripped naked and waiting the 30 seconds for hot water to come out, you have to accept that everyone's going to see your hairy arse as you run between all the cubicles, trying to find where the water is coming out.

One of the club houses had a newly built bar/restaurant with a lovely balcony overlooking the camp-site. Next to the clubhouse was a little grassy area where the little ones were having a kick about. There were no other grown ups playing with them, so I thought I'd be the cool dad and with LJ we joined the game. It's only when playing football with five, six and seven year olds that my footy skills are given the respect they deserve, and I'm recognised as one of the best players on the pitch.

I used the textbook dad approach of stand still as much as possible, kick the ball as far as possible and let them do all the running about. When I did get near their goal, in one of my rare bursts of energy, all that stood between me and ever-lasting glory, was a little, unsure on his feet, three year old. Thinking I'd impress everyone, I put my foot under the ball and chipped it over his little head. It smashed straight into his face, he fell over and his nose started gushing blood.

As the only grown up and being responsible, I picked him up and asked where mummy and daddy were, they were only a tent away from the pitch but thank God they hadn't been watching.

Sometimes we also took the easy option, ditched the tent, strapped the bikes to the car and took a weekend break in the forest at CenterParcs.

This was a lovely bike friendly setting with a network of cycle-paths, weaving their way between the giant firs. There were a couple of hotels but the majority of accommodation was self catering forest lodges, a handful were adapted and catered for wheelchair users, that meant Dad could come too.

Mum always made sure that they had nice holidays, Dad really enjoyed the change of scene and we'd had a couple of really good weeks with them in Norfolk and Dorset. There was also a hotel in North London that Mum found, it had all the facilities, medically trained staff and had a choice of day trips into the city to choose from. The problem with their London trips was that where ever they day-tripped, it always became the location for a terror attack or disaster. They visited Westminster just before the attack, The Shard, Borough Market and London Bridge just before the stabbings and Camden Lock Market just before it burnt down. We felt safe in CentreParcs though, because that had already burnt down and been rebuilt, a number of years ago.

The adapted lodges looked exactly the same as the standard and didn't have a hospital atmosphere like some establishments. They provided an additional extra large bedroom to accommodate the wheelchair user and large disabled bathroom, two little touches that matter so much.

The arrival and departure policy meant that cars were only allowed at the lodges on Mondays and Fridays, once the cars were unpacked on arrival, they had to be deposited in the large car park at the site entrance, leaving all the roads around the lodges free for everyone to safely cycle and stroll.

The holiday makers safety was greatly diminished when Dad was let loose and given the controls to his chair. His wheelchair was an amazing piece of engineering, it was motorised and with the push of a button he could switch from sitting to laying almost flat and even to standing.

When driving along it was usually controlled from a joystick behind the chair by either Mum or myself. There was the option to switch control to the joystick on the armrest up front for Dad to drive.

When in town or a restaurant, where there are kerbs, cobbles, chairs, tables and ankles to navigate, he'd be deadly, but in the middle of the forest, on smooth kerb free tarmac, he could zoom off to his hearts content. If he was approaching anyone, he knew to press the horn and an embarrassing little electronic buzzer would sound, warning people ahead of impending danger.

If we were giving Dad control, we'd make sure the speed setting was the lowest of the three and we'd all follow along behind chatting. He'd drive off in-front, enjoying his freedom, actually being in control of something, then he'd stop and wait for us to catch up, then zoom off again.

The problem was when we chatted and got distracted, one time LJ suddenly said, 'Where's Grandad?' We looked up and he'd driven round the bend ahead and out of view. I'd forgotten to change the speed to the slowest setting.

LJ ran up to the crest of the bend, shouting back that he couldn't see him, we all quickened our pace, rounding the bend and up-to a crossroads 100 yards ahead.
Looking left nothing, right nothing, we could see he wasn't straight ahead, so Boo and LJ went left and me and Mum went right. We went as far as we could, still being able to see each other, but nothing. Then we heard a distant buzz from his horn, Boo shouted he's over here. We ran back to them, 'Where is he? 'We haven't seen him, but the horn came from over there!'
Boo pointed to an expanse of forest, a couple of seconds passed, then there was another buzz, we ran forward, it was definitely him.
We stopped again, listening, like Apache tracking a buffalo, eyes scouring the gaps between the trees, all of a sudden I saw him. He was driving back the way we'd just come from, but on the other side of the river. We could see a bridge in the distance, he must have crossed, all four of us started running in the wrong direction as Dad drove further and further away.

We crossed the bridge and doubled back in the direction he'd gone, out of view again, a cycling couple stopped and asked us if we were looking for a man with a beard in a wheel chair, informing us he'd just turned left towards the tennis courts. We got to the corner and there he was stopped, with his back to us watching an old couple playing tennis. I got up to him, looked at his face and he was pissing himself laughing, the little shit! We switched control to the back of the chair, and composed ourselves.

When Dad was behaving, the whole atmosphere around the lodge and village was very relaxing. There were deer and squirrels to entertain LJ and Dad and if you left your patio door open, you could expect to walk in on a Peacock in your living room, watching the telly.

As well as the swimming pool and sports complex, the main village had a plethora of eating establishments. There were Burger Bars, Italian Style, French Style, Fake Pub Style and Indian. Some dotted around the village, with others accessed from covered atriums and communal lobby areas.

I'd been a few times before but never even looked at the Indian restaurant, it was situated on a mezzanine level, up a sweeping staircase from one of the courtyards with giant cheese-plants. It even had its own little lift that only went up the one level, to just outside the entrance of the Curry House.

LJ and I were just milling around the village, waiting for some reason, trying to amuse ourselves. Everywhere was very quiet, not a sole about, I suggested we go up and look at the Indian restaurant. It was all very plush, there were a couple of fake, illuminated material flames, dancing above the staircase with spotlessly clean carpets. We poked our head around the door, it had a big empty Asian feel to the place and that lovely smell, just as you'd expect.

As we were going to descend the staircase, I spotted a trio of shuffling elderly ladies making their way across the atrium towards the lift. Obviously slowing their pace to that of the oldest one. I assumed she was the mother of the other two, she must have been knocking on 90.

The stage was perfectly set, an empty lift, LJ and I at one end
and we knew who'd be at the other when the doors opened.
I pressed the button and explained the plan to LJ. The doors
opened straight away and it was spotless, the plush carpet,
polished steel handrails with mirrors behind, nothing like the
multi-storey car park toilet lifts you get used to.

We got in and quickly we assumed the crash position, LJ was
opposite me with crumpled legs, hanging on to his handrail.
I was laying on the floor, right leg on my handrail, as the lift
gently came to rest we both let out an Arggghhh!

The doors slowly slid open and the three old ladies just stood
there, open mouthed, staring down at us for a few seconds.
The dominant daughter, still steadying her frail mum, said,
'You're Fucking kidding me!'
We dusted ourselves off, got up, and as we walked past them
towards the exit. I said,
'It's fine on the way up, but coming down is a bit urgent.'
I think I'd embarrassed LJ a bit but at least I'd made myself
laugh.

The ability to make yourself laugh, is a talent that I find very
rarely in others and one I'm extremely proud of. I think I
inherited it from my Dad, he was a musician at heart and had a
recording studio at home, where he spent a lot of his spare time.

His main job was very sensible and boring to me, dealing with
maritime insurance, he was a section head in charge of eight to
ten people. The desks were all pushed together with him sitting
at the head, the others either side facing each other.

In his recording studio he made a cassette for his colleagues. It
was blank for the first 30 minutes, then the sound of some feint
knocking, then a few minutes of silence. Then more knocking
and a little voice,

'Help! Help! Let me out! Let me out!'
At first this was very quiet, but after a few minutes it repeated, getting louder and louder.

He got to work early before everyone else, started the cassette player in his briefcase and put it under the desks where his section sat. Obviously after half an hour the noises started and everyone was wondering where it was coming from. A completely disproportionate amount of time to spend on his comedy tape, but at least he'd made himself laugh.

He justified all the money he spent on his recording equipment, by writing songs too. I thought they were good and he had few contacts in the music industry that gave his skills gravitas. He knew Shakin' Stevens' manager and his pianist, who appeared in his videos, played on some of Dad's songs. Shakey recorded one of Dad's songs but it never made it to the album.

He got to record in the same studio that Madness used and he did get a song on a famous Irish crooners album. This crooner was quite big in the 60s and had a number three single, only being kept off top spot by The Beatles and Rolling Stones. He received a few royalty cheques for a couple of years, not life changing but still 'a thing.'

When you wrote a song back in the day, you had to send a tape of it back to yourself, dated Special Delivery, leaving the envelope seal unbroken, I think as proof for copyright reasons. I found where Dad kept all these unopened padded envelopes in his desk. I didn't know about keeping them sealed and unopened, so I opened most of them. He wasn't happy, but still didn't lose his temper.

One year we were unloading the car after our two week holiday in Switzerland. There were the four of us and Nanny Car. She had only been invited because she didn't drink and it meant Mum and Dad could bring home an extra 12 bottles of wine with her allowance. It was a long journey with three adults and two children, all the luggage and 36 bottles of wine, all sardined into a three door VW Polo.

We were all thinking, 'shame it's all over, but nice to be home,' when Dad turned the excitement up a notch. He'd opened the holiday pile of post on the door mat and had won a Colour TV/Radio/Cassette player. Unbeknownst to us, he'd entered a competition on the radio to do a radio jingle for Ipswich Plastics and won. From then on there was no stopping him.

He became friends with local radio DJs, and the demand for his jingle writing skills just grew and grew. He did adverts for Car Dealers, Stationery Shops, Restaurants, Garden Centres and Burger Bars.

No one in 1970s Ipswich worth talking to wouldn't remember, 'Come on down and taste the size, of Big Daddy's Burger and Fries!' That was one of his.

One day after school on a Wednesday, Dad asked me if I wanted to see the mighty Ipswich Town play, kick-off was at 7.30. This was unheard of, he'd taken me to a home match quite a few times, but never on a mid week school night. I jumped at the chance, Pip had no interest in football, so it was a chance to spend some quality blokey time with my Dad.

Dad was famous for being early for the boat before, the boat before the one we were booked on, so true to form we arrived to a half empty stadium in plenty of time. The atmosphere was nothing like a Saturdays but still an atmosphere. We'd taken our seats in the Pioneer Stand at the Portman Road Theatre of Dreams.

After five minutes, over the Tannoy came the familiar sound of Dad's voice doing one of his adverts. I was so embarrassed, usually it's a radio audience I cant see or just me listening to his latest offering. Now there were thousands, I could see all their faces, all having to listen to Dad's advert. I looked up at him, frowning my disapproval, he was beaming from ear to ear. 'Good isn't it?' He smiled, 'It's going to get better, at half time they're playing one of my songs!'

It took a while for me to forgive him, but he did take me on a works coach to the 1978 FA Cup Semi-Final at Highbury. We beat West Brom that day, going on to beat Arsenal in a glorious final, Roger Osborne scoring the winner in the 77th minute!

As well as his own songs and jingles, Dad recorded songs written by local songwriters, who didn't have their own studio. There was Mr Little, a gold medallist tailor that wrote Christian songs, Mrs Morgan with her organ, an old lady who favoured the Hymn and Jack, he wore a cowboy hat and wrote Country and Western.

The coolest though was when he had bands over to record in his studio. I was 11 or 12 and we had all these punk bands doing their thing, shaking the house with their discordant brilliance and filling the air with fags, beer and whiskey.
We used to watch them from the top of the stairs through the bannisters, with their spiked and spray painted mohawks, smoking and drinking on our doorstep.

The local council villagers, usually only ever seen when the 'Best Kept Village' judging was immanent, reminding us to mow our front lawns, did kick up a fuss. It seems that one band were spotted in the graveyard opposite our house, taking some publicity pics. All of them wearing toilet seats around their necks, the blokes were mooning and the girls simulating sex with a gravestones.

In the swinging sixties when Dad was in a band, they used to drive their Bedford van up to one end of Chelmsford High Street, one of them would get out and start walking, the others drove off. They went round the block and back to the start of the High Street, then drove along slowly until they saw their mate walking.

They screeched to a halt next to him, the other three would get out, throw a blanket over his head and bundle him into the back of the van in a fake kidnapping. All this just to see if anyone reported it to the police. Comedy gold.

Even now sitting in his chair, not being able to create the mischief I know he wants to, he still has the same sense of humour, I can see it in his eyes. I was visiting him and Mum, she was in the kitchen making something tasty for tea, me and Dad were chewing the fat in the lounge, kids TV was on, we weren't really watching but I noticed they seemed to be making spooky food for childrens Halloween parties.

The girl had just made some quite realistic eyeballs from hard boiled eggs and was now fingering a Frankfurter. She got a knife and a centimetre from the end, cut a thin sliver from the sausage, leaving a horseshoe shape, very reminiscent of a fingernail, it looked really good and dad agreed.

A month or so later, I was visiting again, just popping in for a coffee, Mum said if I hear the someone at the door, it'll be Dads Chiropodist. When Dad was first ill with meningitis in France, his second and third toes on his left foot went black and he had to have them amputated, leaving a void between his thumb toe and the two little ones. I reminded Dad of the fake Halloween fingers we'd watched, suggesting we play a joke on the Chiropodist. He completely understood and agreed to me doing it.

Mum didn't have Frankfurters but did have an opened pack of cocktail sausages in the fridge, between the cheese and yoghurt, just behind half a banana wrapped in cling-film. I got two sausages and a knife and took them in to Dad, so he could see what I was doing.

Cutting them like the girl did on telly, to be honest my ones looked even more realistic than the Frankfurters, they weren't so red and where the skin was cut away, the toenail was even better. Dad was wearing sandals which was perfect, I pushed the two little sausages under the sandal strap, into the gap between his toes and he giggled because they were cold.

They looked fucking brilliant, Dad couldn't see down there so I took a picture on my phone to show him, he was crying with laughter.

Dad had spent the 60s squashing his very wide feet into pointy Beatle boots, so they weren't that pretty when he had a full compliment of toes. Mum walked past twice not noticing, just wondering why we were giggling.

The Chiropodist came and had only just knelt down to remove dads sandals, when he recoiled backwards to standing, shouting, 'What the Fuck!'
Me and Dad were pissing ourselves like little schoolboys and to complete the analogy, Mum rushed in and told us both off, my only defence was that Dad told me I was allowed to!

I have nothing but respect and admiration for that man, he made me who I am today. I wont have a bad word said against him and I'd defend him to the hilt. You have to stick up for your Dad, because he stuck up for you!

14 Vagina

As you grow older and your son starts to grow in both stature and confidence, you get excited about his future and the life choices he has to take as they approach.

He overtook the Grandparents years ago and now looms, like a muscle bound Colossus over his mum. The only things smaller than his mum in photos these days are Stanley Schnauzer and things that are a long way away.

I may have immense pride in how my little boy has grown into my big, little boy, but I still miss when he was the little infant information sponge, a time when he couldn't even afford his own iPhone. That tiny, sweet little unbroken voice, that used to call me from upstairs when I was making his sandwiches.
'Daddy, can you wipe my bum?'
I still have my own bum to wipe and take great pleasure in doing so, but you don't get that, being needed, feeling.
Another time I heard an excited
'Daddy Look!' Coming from his room.
I was expecting the usual,
'Daddy Look! I put my bogey on a pencil!' Or
'Daddy Look! I can pull my willy really long!'

This time he looked really excited, pointing out of his window.
I went to the window and there, flying over the houses was a
massive hot air balloon.
'That's a hot air balloon,' I told him.
He said, 'I know it's a balloon Daddy, but who's holding the
string?'

When he was very young our parenting skills surpassed my
expectations, LJ had survived the baby-grow and nappy years,
and we had parental policy issues to deal with. The one where
you had to agree on, what do we call body parts?

I was quite happy with Willy for a Boy's and Front Bottom for
a Girl's. But I really didn't think he'd need to know about girl's
anatomy for a number of years. My wife thought if you're going
to educate your child you should be factual and do it properly.
The offering she brought to the table was Penis and Vagina!
I tried to counter with a more child friendly, Winky and PeePee
for boys parts, FooFoo and Flower for girls, but she was having
none of it. Might as well call it Cock and Fanny I thought.

On the weekend just after, we had a family trip to Tropical
Wings, a sweet little Butterfly Farm near Chelmsford. It was a
good day out, some of the butterflies were massive, quadruple
the size of anything native, a good selection of birds and a few
farm animals, perfect entertainment for little LJ.

We'd seen just about everything and rounded the day off with
the promised milkshake and cake in the coffee shop. We all
knew what we wanted, loaded the trays, one with coffees, one
with our cakes. LJ was in charge of pushing the cakes towards
the till. We stopped and waited our turn, as the purses came out.

10 seconds of inactivity was too much for LJ, he went off
and did his little dance, then he stopped, his face changed to
thoughtful, his brain was ticking I could tell.

He strode straight up to his mum, pointed straight to her crotch and in the loudest voice said,
'Mummy, Is that your Vagina Mummy?'
I was so proud of him. I said
'You take him outside, I'll pay.' It was the least I could do.

At a later date, I heard of another butterfly place in the same area called Flappy Flaps. If only I'd known then, I could have had that as one of my naming options.

One of the favourite perks afforded you, when you own a toddler, is unquestioned access to soft play areas. In my day we climbed trees, played on building sites and in fields, threw stones, got hit by stones and went home hurting and bleeding, but happy.

Now the little ones have the free reign of entire warehouses, padded all over with toboggan slides and ball pits. Our local one even has a football pitch suspended 20ft high up in the scaffolding.

When they're under two it can be a bit frustrating, you get a tiny ball pit, not much bigger than your paddling pool at home, a few padded shapes and maybe a Wendy house. It entertains the little ones, but the dads are itching to get into the big padded labyrinth and show the bigger kids how to really have fun.

After the toddler area, the next zone is limited to five year olds, it has a decent 10ft slide into a brilliant ball pit, deep enough for the dads to hide under the surface. I could spend hours in there pissing about, we took great pleasure sitting there, chest deep in little plastic balls, telling 8 to 10 year olds to get out because they were too big.

Another of my little man's achievements was to successfully fill his sleeves with badges gathered in the Scout movement, the first in my family to do so. It was never offered to me as an option and my Dad got kicked on his first day for smoking.

He had a couple of years being a Beaver, then at seven, he was too old and graduated to the Cubs. This of course meant a trip to the Scout shop for his new uniform, a little wooden building behind the Secondary school.

It was manned or womanned by an old, rotund, jolly lady, dressed I think as Brown Owl, her sleeves full of badges and a neckerchief secured by the finest woggle.

LJ and his mum were collecting all the newly branded Cub sweatshirts, scarfs and hats he needed, while I aimlessly wandered the shelves browsing and keeping out of the way.

I spotted in the girls section, little tiny sweatshirts, all neatly folded with Rainbows across the front. I asked the rotund lady behind the till what Rainbows were?
She replied, completely straight faced,
'They're like Little Girls Beavers.'

I have always been a person, that often criticised, would talk to anyone. I wanted to pass my confidence on to LJ so that he was happy speaking to adults and people in authority, whether they were a Teacher, Shopkeeper or Policeman.

No one likes the cocky little twat you often see gobbing off to everyone, but equally frustrating to me, are the timid little frightened kids that cower behind their parents legs, like a regularly beaten puppy, too afraid to interact with anything that isn't made of Lego! Probably a Vegan!

One Saturday it was just LJ and me going into town, we walked holding hands from the car park up to the high street. We waited at the zebra crossing for the green man, the same crossing that 20 years earlier, a little old lady fell in-front of my car and everyone thought I'd hit her.

The green man beeped his permission and as we crossed, I saw a situation present itself to me that I couldn't resist. Right in front of us was the party shop, where you get all your party favours, jokes and birthday number balloons. In front of the party shop window was a Traffic Warden just standing there, hands behind his back, surveying any drivers stopping at the taxi rank in front.

LJ and I walked straight up to him and I quite politely said, 'Sorry Mate, you can't stay there, I want to look at the party balloons, can you move along please?'
He apologized and took a couple of steps to the left.
We looked for a moment then walked off, I said thank you to him as we left. Teaching LJ that you can talk to anyone, as long as you're polite.

We are lucky where we live in North Essex, it's a lovely part of the country that most people don't know about. It is nothing like the fake tits and teeth of TOWIE Essex, or the Asian smuggling Estuary Essex.

Colchester is England's oldest town, sure we have more than our fair share of murders, but we've got a Castle and a Zoo too. We're also only 10 minutes from 'Constable Country,' with Flatford and Dedham providing the inspiration for many a famous painter.

We were on the way to Flatford, a tiny hamlet, home to Willy Lott's Cottage that features in the Hay Wain. We'd been on the rowing boats many times before but this was the first time that we were letting LJ and his friend Mash take a boat out on their own. He was very excited.

We wandered down to the little hump back bridge where

the boats were hired. The Fella in charge was a right cocky comedian, as all the kids were boarding the boats, he was giving everyone girl's names.

Mash and LJ got in the number 13, he said,
'There you go Kylie, there you go Tracey, do you want a little ducky?' Offering them a plastic duck on a piece of string to tow. They tutted and sitting down said, 'Na, you're alright.'

They had their half hour and we watched from the bridge and alongside on the riverbank. They docked and when disembarking Mr. Funny asked,
'Alright Kylie, Alright Tracey was that fun?'
They said 'Yeah.' Then they asked, 'What's your name then?'
'Oh I can't tell you that… but I'll tell you it starts with a D.'
They both went 'Oh' and walked past him, as LJ got level, with perfect comedic timing, no eye contact, he just said, 'Dick!' And walked off.

At 11 years old and in his final year at primary school, LJ announced to us that, next week his class was going to do sex education! I couldn't believe it, my primary teacher Eunice would never even mention the word sex. I doubt she knew what it was herself, being such a hideous, objectionable, man hating bitch!
If she ever did experience a real penis, there wasn't a man on earth that could mentally persuade his blood to engorge it with her in the room, to create anything even approaching an erection, I doubt even a lazy lob!

It wasn't until my third year at secondary school, when science split into Physics, Chemistry and Biology, that we had sex education. All the boy's Biology books fell open at page 56, this was where a pen and ink drawing of a penis entered a pen and ink vagina.

The lesson was an anti climax, the teacher said nothing, a lab assistant in a brown lab coat wheeled the telly and video in and pressed play. The best thing that happened the whole lesson was when Nancy feinted and fell off her chair. It was funny when the teacher and school nurse were seeing to her, with the sex tape carrying on above their heads. Funny too that Nancy was the girl rumoured to give 50p blow-jobs behind the youth club.

When LJ was dropped off at school, he or his mates didn't really seem that bothered. I think I was more excited to hear what happened.

When I picked him and two friends up after school, I asked if Miss Smith did the sex talk, he said that she did just the girls and Mr. Meathrill the teaching assistant did the boy's talk.
'Well, what did you learn?' I asked.
'We did learn that a lady uses a Dildo to pleasure herself.'
I was gob-smacked,
'Why on earth would he tell you that?'
'It was when we asked questions at the end, Ben asked what a Dildo was.'
'How would he know about Dildos?' I asked.
'He uses one to kill people in Grand Theft Auto! He wanted to know what it was.'

15 France

When we were expecting little LJ, the time was approaching when traditionally you could tell people, I don't think anyone knew and we obviously thought that our parents should be first. We decided on a two-pronged attack, each of us would go and tell our respective parents individually, then neither of them would be the first to know.

Our siblings had already furnished each of them with a Grandchild already, so it wasn't their first and we weren't expecting a brass band, fireworks or even tears. I was expecting a bit of interest though, I thought it might even be the main subject of conversation over Sunday lunch.

After I told Mum and Dad in the kitchen, expecting them to be all excited about having a new baby to play with, they too had their own bombshell news.

They had both recently taken early retirement, the house was all paid for and they were going to France for a couple of months, to find a place to live! Great I thought, that cuts our number of baby sitters by 50%.

They had booked a selection of Gites over the two months in

different parts of Burgundy. Eventually finding a lovely place just North of Macon, on the main route to the Mediterranean.

Mum and Dad were still in this country when LJ was born and had a few months to bond, but then, like Keyser Söza…They were gone!

It was over a year before I saw their new house, obviously having a new baby was filling our itinerary. The first time I went over was when I got a call from Mum, saying that Dad was in the hospital with Meningitis.

I left for France early hours the next day and was there by mid afternoon. She was all alone and having to deal with all the hospital shite in French, the one who was fluent in French was laying in a coma for six weeks.

Over the next few years I had numerous trips over to France and more often than not, I always seemed to attract the attention of customs.

Usually travelling alone, my easiest option was driving onto a train and going through the Chunnel. I tried the Eurostar a couple of times but was always stopped going out by customs.

The two things Mum has always been addicted to were Cheddar Cheese and Tea, neither of which are readily available to her in France. My case was usually a third full of my clothes and toiletries and two thirds Cheese and Tea. Twice custom officers pulled me aside on the Eurostar, I was very close to missing the train both times.

I had 13 large blocks of strong Cheddar and over 500 tea bags. The problem was when my case went through the X-ray machine the Cheddar raised the alarm bells because evidently, it has a similar density to Cemtex.

The worst though was when I was delivering a powered wheelchair from England, that Mum had bought on the internet from France. My Dad had been in various hospitals for over a year and was now home with my Mum. This chair was brilliant, a really comfy multi positional seat and powered wheels, so mum didn't have to push. It changed from sitting to either laying completely flat or fully standing. This would really help his recovery with things like blood flow and up to a point, his independence.

On the way to France, the chair was nearly disassembled at customs, but that was nothing compared to the return journey.

In Mum's garden she had inherited the largest, most loved Walnut tree in the village. I don't like Walnuts myself but these were very impressive, approaching the size of a tangerine and I'm told by everyone who tried them, the best they'd ever had.

So much so, that with it's first years droppings came a queue of local villagers, knocking on the gates enquiring about the crop. Evidently the previous custodian of the tree used to allow locals to help themselves to as many as they wanted, there were just so many nuts.

It was true, they were ankle deep under the tree and rolling for yards down the hill. On the day I left for home we filled two wheelbarrows full. The previous day Mum had filled all the boxes she had and three plastic dustbins.

I still had the back seats of the car down to accommodate the wheelchair and cheese I'd brought her, all the space was now filled on the return journey with two plastic dustbins, five large boxes all full Walnuts and about 30 bottles of wine.

The wine bottles were chinking together every time anything was put in the car, I knew this would really piss me off on the way to Calais. I unpacked some dirty T-shirts and clean pants and put them between the bottles, but there were too many bottles and not enough pants.

Mum came to the rescue as always, she went into the house and came out with a box of Dad's incontinence pants, she said, 'These are perfect because they have sticky fasteners, we can stick them on the bottles.'
A weird idea but it worked perfectly.

At Calais as expected, I was pulled over, but not for a quick once over as usual, this time I was directed to a white specially lit garage with six boiler suited inspectors.

I stood just outside the garage sparked up a fag and explained my situation to a nice female officer. I told her about Mum's tree and that all the Walnuts were for friends and family back home.

Then as they opened the boot, I thought Shit! I had to explain why the wine was wrapped in pants and adult nappies. She said not to worry, they've seen worse. I thought they must be nearly finished, but then I saw the front seats come out and put next to the car.

They swarmed over the car like fruit flies over a fresh turd. The nuts were being emptied into massive plastic trays. They were tapping panels, wiping door handles and on their backs under the car with torches. I was getting worried now, I'd only had the car for three months, what if the previous owner had drugs in the car or explosives? They might pick up a trace.

Then things seemed to get serious, my sphincter tightened as one inspector called another over, he then called another. They seemed to be concentrating on the dashboard. After what seemed ages, one of them strode over to me, and asked, 'Did you have the air-conditioning working on the way here?'
I said, 'Yes.'
'It seems that the fan doesn't appear to be working Sir.'
I thought 'They must suspect a drugs blockage.'
I said that it was working an hour ago, it was over 30 degrees so I remember having it on.

I was preparing myself for the worst. In a minute my belt will be undone, my trousers would be around my ankles and my anal cherry was about to be popped by the gloved fingers of a Customs Official.

I was just about to request that the nice lady I was talking to before, be the one to invade my virgin arse-hole, when one of the monkeys called across,
'Pete You Twat! The ignition has to be on for the blower to work. It's working fine.'

Within minutes they seemed to be done with me, they'd rebuilt my car, reloaded it and I was free to drive onto the carriage and finally head home.

16 Cock

Before my wife was even showing in her early pregnancy months, we like everyone had to prepare the nursery. I had my office in the smallest bedroom and that had been earmarked for LJ's nursery. I knew that becoming a father I'd have to make some sacrifices, so without any objection I packed everything up and moved to the second bedroom. I really didn't mind, it was much bigger and I'm sure she was doing a lot harder work building a baby.

It was a great house, a three bedroom link detached with an integral car port, exactly the same as our neighbours just handed. I pulled up under the car port one day and my next door neighbour was cleaning his car. He said,
'I see you're moving your office to the big room, when's the baby due?' I asked how he could possibly know, he said that it was exactly what he was made to do the year before, when they dropped their first.

We were preparing the house for the baby, but knew in the back of our minds that we really needed something with a bit more garden. At the moment we were settling for our small courtyard garden that we'd completely paved, not very child friendly.

Our hands were easily forced a couple of months later, when our neighbours put their near identical house on the market for nearly £250k, over three times what we'd both paid for our new-builds. We hadn't a clue they were worth so much, we were so used to dealing with negative equity with our first home that we forgot house prices go up too. We were soon on the market and looking ourselves.

We found a characterful 15th Century cottage with a detached 20th Century garage, ample parking and a well-established private garden with several massive mature trees.
The lady that owned the adjoining cottage lived in Switzerland and hadn't been back for years. The woman selling the house had only seen her once in four years, so no attached neighbours.

She also told us a little about the house, it used to be an Inn called The Cock and it's history was documented in a book written by a local author, she did have a copy but it went into storage when they de-cluttered for viewings.

A few years later when taking LJ to the library, I remembered mention of the book and found it in the reference section, I wasn't allowed to borrow it so I photocopied the relevant pages that referred to our house.

When reading it later, it revealed that in recent renovations the skeleton of a young girl was revealed behind the fire place in the North wing, before it was divided into three cottages. I checked on my phone compass and as I thought, it was in our house. Probably why we weren't shown the book before buying.

One thing that sold the house to me, was the proximity of the Swan Inn over the road. It too dated back to the 15th Century but had always remained an Inn. Funny enough, it was where me and the wife to be had our first date eight years before.

In my college days it was always the place to 'Grab a Granny' on Thursday nights. A regular watering hole for young mums before they poured themselves down the road to 'Ladies Night' at the Windmill Nightclub.

Nowadays the food was good and it had retained its oldie-worldy beamed pub feel. The Swan's reputation for its good food, meant that when we invited some close relatives and their kids over to see the new house, we could be confident about the service and menu.

We showed them around the house then walked over the road to the pub, where we had booked a table. As we approached we were hit by a massive shock. There standing at the entrance to the car park was a newly erected pub sign, as if someone was having a joke at our expense were the dreaded words, Hungry Horse.

As we approached the front door, we could hear the microwaves pinging though the kitchen window, like fruit machines in a Southend arcade.

We were looking forward to some tasty home cooked fare from the chef's fine hands, instead we ended up with a selection of under and over microwaved frozen food, thrown together by a bunch of job-seekers from the DHS, no experience needed.

The funniest thing we saw was a specialty of the house, or Horse. The table next to us, a young family, had ordered Onion Rings with Dips. These came piled on a broom handle nailed to an old bread board and stood about three feet tall, very stylish.

I patronised the pub a couple of times after that with my mate Steppy when Liverpool were playing in Europe, they had Sky Sports, but we never went in there to eat again.

A few years later my car was out of action for a couple of days and I had to be a 'Bus Wanker'. The bus stop was right in front of the Swan, and for a week it had been closed, the whole car

park had been surrounded by metal building site fencing. As I
was waiting for the bus a painter came out from the pub with
splattered overalls, he went to the back of his van then headed
back to the pub carrying two big tins of paint.

I called him over and through the fence asked him if he knew
what the plans for the pub were. We were obviously hoping it
was under new management and would return to its previous
independent state.
'Is it under new management or are they just refurbishing it?'
I asked.
'Just repainting,' he replied, 'same owners, nothing's changing.'
'Oh Shit, never mind.'
'Why Oh Shit?' He said,
'Well,' I replied, 'It's just one of those Hungry Horses isn't it,
used to be really nice but now it's all shit microwaved food and
Onion Rings on broom handles. Everyone's hoping it had new
owners and going back to like it used to be.'

The painter looked at me a little dejected, like he'd taken more
offence to my comments than a painter should. Then the penny
dropped. I said,
'You're not just a painter are you?'
'No,' he replied, 'I'm the Landlord… I'll take your comments on
board.' He walked off.

In the opposite direction to the pub, which I don't mind being
so close, is an out of town shopping development, partly
blamed for the slow, painful death of the High Street. It's two
minutes drive away and close enough to be handy, far enough
away that we can't smell all the chicken and burgers frying at
Cholesterol Corner.

My favourite shop is Sainsbury, I feel I'm in there more often
than not and it's like a second home. I think I do more hours

in there than some of the staff, I know most of them to talk to and which ones not to bother with.

This made it quite embarrassing on a couple of occasions. I'd lost a bit of timber and threw on a clean pair of jeans in a hurry, not bothering with a belt. I'd filled my basket with liquids, eight cans of beer, a bottle of wine, Actimel, to aid my bacterial transit and a Toilet Duck, it was very heavy, then I remembered toilet rolls.

As the last thing to get on the way to the tills, I got a big pack of 16 and tucked them under my free arm. I turned a corner and thankfully had an unpopulated aisle all to myself. Halfway along, not gradually, but in a second, my trousers deserted my waistline and found my ankles. I flew forward in slow motion with the basket crashing to the ground, a can of beer split and was Katherine wheeling its frothy contents across the floor. Luckily I didn't drop the toilet rolls, they cushioned by fall as I fell on top.

I got up and just as I'd re-covered my modesty, a supervisor poked her head around the end of the aisle to see what the commotion was. I think I got away with that one.

The next time my trousers fell down, a little old lady saw but I managed to catch them at the knees and I didn't fall over! These embarrassments pale into insignificance compared with my best moment.

I was walking towards the toilet roll aisle, just after the baby items and before the pet food. As I walked past the own brand packs of SuperSoft, I approached a woman about my age that did an enormous sneeze! To make the situation even better, she was standing next to a vicar dressed in black, complete with dog collar.
She sneezed, I said very politely, 'Bless you!'
The Vicar turned his head, and I said jokingly,
'You should have said that, it's not my job.'

Vic looked at me and just said, 'Oh, Sod Off!'

Other shops in the area, provide a great many options if I'm bored and have an hour or three to waste.

Argos is always a go to. It has lost its identity a bit when they waved goodbye to the laminated catalogue, but I can still entertain myself with the new system. You have to place your order on a plumbed-in iPad and provide a memorable word that the person on the till has to say. Obviously I tried to input Fuck, Shit, Wank, Tit, Cunt, Bum and Arsehole, but the programmers had thought someone might and blocked them. Swallow, Tickle, Perineum, Wibble and Gobble did work.

B&M Bargains was coming to our side of town, everyone was waiting for this bargain basement store to open. Our side had never lowered itself to accept the unbranded German style venders or the 'Everything for a Quid' approach.

It was a novelty and I really wanted to have a look around, a bit like staying in a five star hotel in Rio, but still wanting a tour of the corrugated-roofed Favelas on the hillside.

I was lucky enough to be their first ever customer through the door. The massive sign was now up and the doors were open, it seemed quiet but I had to go see what all the fuss was about. I grabbed one of their brand new virgin baskets and perused the aisles. Taking my time, I spotted some well known brands and some were indeed a lot cheaper than Sainsburys.

I basketed a couple of tins of Ravioli, a giant HP Sauce and Tommy Ketchup, I'd already saving about three quid and was only in aisle one. Around the first corner were Biscuits and Shampoo, some Dried Pasta and a bottle of Wine for £2.99. Next aisle, a three litre bottle of Tramp Cider, two bottles of Squash and a multipack pack of Tissues, I was on a roll. End of aisle two, I spotted nine Toilet Rolls for £1.99 right next to the Perfume, just before the Solar Powered Glowing Garden Frog Lights.

I was half way up aisle three with a Dove deodorant roll-on in my hand, thinking that I must have saved over a tenner already, when I was approached by what looked like a 12 year old with a moustache. He had an assistant manager name tag proudly pinned to his chest.

He explained to me that the shop wasn't actually opening until Friday in two days, they were still getting ready. I felt a bit stupid, he said I didn't have to put the things back on the shelves, he'd sort it. So I had to leave and wait till the weekend.

On the rare occasion I treat LJ to a Mc Meal, he has to suffer me putting on the campest, most gender fluid voice I can muster into the drive-through microphone. After everything I order, there's a
'Ohhhhhh I really want some meat big boy!' Or, 'See Ya at the window Sweetie!'
LJ cowers in his seat as we approach the payment window and I change back to normal. 'Cheers Mate, thanks a lot!' In my butchest voice.

17 Boo

As I pass through life with it nearing its end. In the Autumn of my years, well late Autumn early Winter, end of November just coming into December, I wonder where all the Summers went. Will I ever see the hope in and approach of another Spring?

I sit alone, contemplating my navel, I realise the one thing that has been a constant in my life over the last 25 years is my Boo. A fine figure of a woman when I married her and now a fine figure of a 20 year older woman.

She has in those years, taken what God has gifted her and with the help of Vegetarianism, Step Aerobics, Yoga and Weights now has the body of a boy half her age.

Still turning heads and encouraging amazed double-takes from strangers, when she waxes lyrical of her memories from the 70s and 80s. She just doesn't look old enough.

In our time together, it is Boo who has been the chewing gum in my hair, sticking everything together. My Asbestos shield, protecting me from the extreme temperatures of life, and the nagging Air Traffic Control voice of doubt in my head, keeping me grounded.

Yes she is multi skilled, as an Editor she can write, proof-read, spell, punctuate and ensure a house style is being adhered to. As a trained Beauty Therapist she can still cut and style a head of hair and be complimented by her peers. She can paint nails and wax a bikini line with the best of them.
As an orator she is eloquent and skilled and as a mother she is unsurpassed. But, she does have her moments and circumstances have hindered her in the past.

When she was a Beauty Therapy student, the college doors were open to human guinea pigs who didn't mind students practicing on them for a small contribution.

She was in the middle of a practical exam, Boo had a nice Indian lady who'd agreed to partake in a pedicure. First her feet were washed, massaged and her toenails trimmed, just as her examiner came to watch, the Indian ladies big toenail boomeranged from her foot and landed smack bang in the middle of Boo's bottom lip. Not being able to spit it out or express any disgust, she left the little crusty crescent, sitting on her lip until the examiner passed.

The thing that holds her back at certain times, is her own lack of joined up thinking. Boo and I had been driving along with LJ who was only little, when Boo said as an excited mother, 'Look LJ, lots of sheep in that field!'
LJ looks, I look, LJ has a face of confusion, all we can see is straw bales. 'Oh sorry, I thought they were sheep. She said.

One October we all went to the park searching for conkers. Colchester Park has a good selection of Horse Chestnut trees and we were all searching below. All three of us with heads bowed like monks, kicking the leaves around hoping to expose any half open spiky husks. After about five minutes I drew LJ's attention to the fact that his mum had wandered off a little and was now looking for conkers under a Sycamore tree.

We watched her wander under random Oaks and Beech trees and when she started looking under a Monkey Puzzle, we stopped her and took her off for a mug of coffee.

Another time Boo's good intentions proved accidentally an unwanted hindrance to me, was when we were in town. Usually I'm just the mule that carries Boo's purchases, clothes, cushions, candles etc. This time was different, for the first time in months I wanted to buy something and she had to wait for me.

I wanted a CD, Ol' Dirty Bastard's (ODB) album, 'N***a Please'. Due to the title I didn't want to ask for it so started searching the alphabetical CD troughs. As I browsed I sensed her getting fidgety, she wasn't used to waiting for me. She went off somewhere and reappeared minutes later with someone to help find the CD for me.

He was a Massive 6'6 black man with more muscles on his neck than I had in my body.
'What you looking for sir?' He asked.
When I said the ODB CD, he grinned broadly,
'Which one sir?'
He knew which one I wanted I could tell.
'The new one.' I squeaked, 'I don't know what it's called.'
He handed it to me, laughing inwardly, saying, 'Here you go sir.'
He sucked his teeth at me and went.
To be fair to Boo, she didn't know the title.

18 Boot

We woke reluctantly, I looked at the clock and it was showing stupid o'clock in the morning. Today was the day of our first ever car boot sale. It was exciting before I went to bed, but now seemed an unnecessary chore. I suggested as the car was already loaded I could just take it to the tip, then we could lay in! This evidently wasn't an option.

We'd been to a couple of car boot sales, but on the way back from places when we were driving past, this was our first time as actual venders. We'd been warned about the professional 'Booters,' that crowd your car as you arrive, but were still a bit taken back with their eagerness.

It was how I imagined a couple of naked, do-anything Nymphomaniacs would be received as they pulled up in a dark Doggers car park, just before the perverts sea-gulled all over their windscreen.

In the time it had taken us to get out of the car and walk around to the back, they had already opened the boot and were rummaging through our stuff. As friends had instructed us, I shut the boot, locked the doors and we went to the Grease

Wagon to get a coffee. As we were told they would, they all fucked off and started bothering the next car to park up.

The boot sale was being held in a field close to the little market town where I went to school. I was wondering if I'd recognise any old friends, I hadn't really seen anyone for years, since college.

We'd borrowed our temporary shop fittings, an old folding wallpaper pasting table, a small tarpaulin and a hanging rail for Boo's clothes. We emptied the car and displayed all our wares, looking around at similar sellers I didn't think we were going to embarrass ourselves too much.

Sod's law, one of the first people to stop and chat was a girl from my class Sarah, we were friends at school, and went on only one date when I first got my car. She was with her friend and recognised me before I'd realised who she was.

Our date didn't go too well, as she told her friend. We were on our way to Chelmsford to do some shopping. I needed petrol and stopped at the services on the A12 that I'd be working at in a couple of years. I put in a couple of quids worth of petrol, re-holstered the pump and walked to the shop to pay. It was quite busy and I could see a long queue in the shop.

I got half way between the pump and shop, in front of all the cars being filled. I could feel something falling down my trouser leg. I looked down and as I walked I could see the blue Ipswich Town pants that I had been wearing the day before, that Nan had bought me, revealing themselves to the world.

They didn't fall out, just flapped around my ankle to make sure everybody could see. I quickly tugged them free and put them in my pocket. All this on the one day that I'd made sure my pants were clean and my best pair.

We were selling quite a bit of stuff, I was happy to see the back of a couple of old mirrors, a cot bed and a 1950s radio from Lily and Stan's house, that'd free a bit of garage space.

Boo's clothes were going quite well, but I think she was a little offended when various scabby travellers, took her designer clothes off the hangers and with their free grubby hand held out a 50p, thinking that'd be deal done.

They were soon wafted away and by early afternoon a better class of bargain hunter appeared, they recognised the labels and were happy to take paper money from their purses.

I had my own encounter with the traveller community, I knew of him and his reputation. He was from an infamous family of scrap dealers, his Nan was rumoured to have stabbed the 'Ma' of another family with a stiletto heel.

I had my selection of paperback books arranged neatly on the table and he was showing an interest. All my books were about gangsters and criminals. He picked up the Tony Lambrianou biography, read the back cover and put it back. He picked up the Krays book, put it back, then he picked up my favourite book, Hard Bastards.

I was just about to tell him that all the books were only 20p when he opened it to the first page. There, still in the book was my make-do bookmark. A photo of me sitting in our Roosevelt Hotel room in New York, in just my boxer shorts, drinking a large glass of brandy! I took the photo and said that it wasn't included, I don't know if that was the deal breaker but he didn't buy the book, just walked off.

The only other person I knew was Craig, he was one of my best mates but only at our school for the last year. He seemed to be with a girl from our class, I can't remember her real name, but I am sure that it was Craig that gave her the nickname 'Jigsaw,' because she was boring and no-one wanted to do her.

Craig's dad had owned a pub in Romford and was told he'd die if he didn't stop drinking, so he sold up and moved to the country.

He was different to us, we were all into Madness, The Specials, The Birthday Party and Joy Division, he came to the table liking Duran Duran, sporting a Phil Oakey haircut, half shaved and half girl. His stories of London and knowledge of Sex was complete bullshit but so funny.

If he saw a horny girl, he'd say his hard-on was like, 'A baby's arm holding a cooking apple!' Or, 'Like a tin of Vim with a sheep's heart on top!'

He also had a library of sexual positions.

The Bucking Bronco - This is when the girl is on all fours and you are penetrating from behind, hugging her tight, after a few minutes you say another girls name, then see how long you can stay on!

The Hot Dog - This is when the girl is on her back, you're straddling her chest receiving a blow-job. Just as she thinks you're going to cum, you do a poo between her tits then push them together!

The Angry Pirate – When receiving a standing blow-job, you make sure you cum in your partners eye, when she stands up to go to the bathroom and clean up, you kick her in the shin. This leaves her with a closed eye, hopping on one leg going, Argggh, Argggh! Like an Angry Pirate.

He also reckoned he'd walked in on his mum 'Gusset Typing.' And his sister 'Flicking her pea into her canoe.' All complete bullshit stories, but very creative and entertaining.

Craig looked a bit rough, the last time I saw him he'd just had a teenage meltdown with his parents, left home and was living in a squat next to Tesco. Now from his complexion and twitchiness, it looked that he was still raging against the machine, but had added Class A to his diet. I didn't think we'd stay in touch.

The crowds were thinning, the customers, immigrants and their thieving children were all departing in their cars and vans, and we were left counting the profit that our car load had earned us. Not bad for a days work and still only three o'clock.

We sorted the things we wanted to keep and the stuff to dump as we reloaded the car, then went home. At home I swapped our thing we were keeping with two large dirty rubble sacks full of leaves and garden waste, and headed to the council tip before it closed.

The tip is only 20 minutes away but the smell in the car from the rotting leaves made me wish it was closer. They had been left in the rain for too long and the muddy stagnant water was leaking badly from holes in the threadbare sacks.

At the tip, they were the first things out of the car, wiping their shitty residue across the front of my jeans as I manhandled them from the boot.

I dragged them up to Skip 5 Garden Waste, when trying to lift it up to waist height to empty it, I covered myself in even more shit, having to brush off two massive slugs trying to escape up my arm.

Glad they were empty I dragged the sacks, still leaking a slimy trail across the car park, just as the slugs had up my sleeve. I walked up to my open boot and threw the bags in, more slugs and mud falling to the carpet and a previously hidden pool of brown juice made itself known, leaking from a hole in the bottom. I had to clean the car anyway so it wasn't a problem.

It just occurred to me that the car boot rubbish had gone, the boot had been empty. I looked up and in the rear foot well was a shiny air canister with plastic tubes coming from the top.

My gaze followed the tubes up to the front seat headrests and into the nostrils of a sunken eyed, grey skinned old man peaking from behind.

I'd got the wrong car, I apologised to the old man and took the bags, quickly retreating to the safety of my car two behind. I had left a hell of a wet, muddy, sluggy mess in his boot but he didn't look like he was well enough to come after me and get aggressive. I ignored the bags that I hadn't dumped and thought it best to get out of there.

As I drove past the old man I realised that our cars weren't even the same colour. His was white, mine is blue, what was I thinking?

19 Poo

With all these memories of all my years, have I reassured myself that it was worth emerging from between my mother's milky thighs, wet and sticky all those years ago?

Was it worth all the effort learning to walk, talk, read and write? Whenever I walk my trousers fall down, whenever I talk I upset someone. Everything I read I upset myself and whatever I write I read it alone.

I'm waiting for my test results, sitting in the corner of the doctors waiting room, my eyes surveying the walls but all I see is a vague kaleidoscope of white rectangles. Since I found my lump my head has been full of cotton wool. I don't know how many days it's been, I don't even know if I've had breakfast, life has just been a blurry mess.

I'm like a tiny lone cloud, floating across an expanse of clear blue sky, no one noticing my existence, affecting no-one's decision as to wear a coat or not, I'm just floating by.

Suddenly, I start giggling to myself, remembering when the Scout lady said that Rainbows were like little girls Beavers.

The blurred rectangles of white shimmied into focus, my eyes cleared and I could read the Bristol Poo Chart on the opposite wall. Wow, it's actually 'Stool Chart' not 'Poo Chart,' I never knew that. Something had made me smile! The numbness was leaving me.

I was like the fumbling, skinny, fly covered African child in the mid-morning charity advert on TV, not the one with the hair-lip, the other one that's had his cataracts removed and now he can see. I read on…

Type 1, Separate hard lumps, like nuts (hard to pass).
Type 2, Sausage-shaped, but lumpy!

Wow, I'm having a moment of clarity, maybe I had enjoyed my life, this was funny, maybe it hadn't been all bad.

Type 3, Sausage-shaped, but with cracks on the surface!

This was brilliant, my mood had been lifted by a Poo chart. I have had a good life!

Who else can say they've moved on a traffic warden?
Who else has had the opportunity to do 'Crash Positions' in a perfectly clean lift? And I bet no-one has ever 'Bless You'd' a woman sneezing, next to a vicar!

I may have only made myself laugh, but at least I laughed! I was quite prepared that the doctor was going to tell me, my bollock lump was going to kill me, I just didn't care.

Just then 'Wendell Gee – Room 3' came on the TV screen with a ding. I took a deep breath, stood up and turned to the corridor on the left. A dead man walking, I took two steps then stopped, I couldn't go any further, the sign on the wall said 'Rooms 4-7'. I turned around and went down the right corridor opposite, towards Room 3.

I knocked on the door and walked in, Dr Maan turned from his screen and said please take a seat. Did he want me to sit because it was bad news? Of course not I thought, he always says take a seat.

'I wont beat around the bush,' he said, 'it's good news, the results are back from the lab and your lump is benign!' He smiled. I knew he said it was good news, but I still had to say in my head 'Benign Good - Malignant Bad.'

I didn't know whether to laugh or cry then my brain just decided for me and I started sobbing like a baby. All I could think was that I would see LJ pass his driving test! My eyes were leaking like an old toilet, my tears falling onto my knees, like Type 7 on the Bristol Stool Chart. Watery, no solid pieces (entirely liquid).

As I slowed my wailing to a breathless sob, he calmly said,

'We think the lump is Chewing Gum.'

I thought for a minute, I do spit chewing gum between my legs when I'm doing a poo. It must have latched onto a testicle hair, swung on the hair and adhered itself to the underside of my scrotum.

I admitted to Dr Maan that I do have a habit of pulling little Gee to the side and spitting my gum into the toilet.

He suggest that I try gently massaging Peanut Butter into my testicles to see if that frees the gum. He said, 'The girls on reception say it works with chewing gum in their daughter's hair and they think it will work on your testicles too!'

Great, now I have to walk past them to get out, I didn't really care, I wouldn't be laughing alone!

It's said that, 'History is written by Winners.' Now my little history has been written, by a Loser?

Wendell done!

Printed in Great Britain
by Amazon

21918484R00086